TRUMP OR CLINTON: HOW WOULD CHRIST VOTE?

TIMOTHY A. JACOBSON
B.S., M.A., J.D., LTC, U.S. ARMY (RET.)

Trump or Clinton: How Would Christ Vote?

Printed in the United States of America.

First Edition.

DEDICATION

This book is hereby dedicated to:

The God of Abraham, the God of our Founding Fathers.
"In Him we live, and move, and have our being"
(Acts 17:28, KJV).

My parents Rev. Gerald and Jean Jacobson,
and brothers Thomas, Michael, and Daniel.

My wife Delores
and daughters Rebecca, Kristin, and Kelsey.

SPECIAL HONOR

On the day that she suffered the final stroke that silenced her forever, my mother was doing what she enjoyed most, quoting Scripture and singing hymns. The words "For to me, to live is Christ and to die is gain" (Phil. 1:20-22) epitomized her life. My father and mother were united in total commitment to loving and serving the Lord until the passing of my mother. Today my father, an 88-year-old retired minister, missionary, and state prison chaplain, continues to work as a hospital chaplain. He is a wonderful father and grandfather, completely devoted to the Lord and to his family.

AUTHOR

Timothy Jacobson is a Christian attorney and retired Army Officer. His academic degrees include a Bachelor of Science, United Stated Military Academy, West Point, Master of Arts in Theology, Summa Cum Laude, Regent University, and Juris Doctor in Law, Regent University. His 33 years of military service included 11 years on active duty and 22 years of National Guard and Reserves.

FAVORITE QUOTES

"For me to live is Christ, and to die is gain."
The Apostle Paul.

"God made me fast, and when I run, I feel His pleasure."
Eric Liddel, Chariots of Fire,
Olympic runner and missionary to China.

"Thanks be to God for the challenge and the victory."
West Point yearbook.

"Help me to never seek a crown, for
my reward is giving glory to you."
Keith Green, songwriter.

TABLE OF CONTENTS

CHAPTER 1.0

INTRODUCTION

MORAL DECLINE, DUTY TO VOTE. Christians bear primary responsibility for the moral decline of our nation. Every Christian has a duty and moral obligation to vote in every election, to vote as Christ would vote, and to support his or her vote with scripture. How would Christ vote in the 2016 election? Would He vote for Trump or Clinton? Would He vote for Republicans or Democrats? This book answers these questions with absolute certainty based upon principles and laws embodied in scripture, the Declaration of Independence, the Constitution, and the Bill of Rights. It provides voter guidance and greater understanding of God, Scripture, and the laws that God created to govern men and nations. It will also challenge your understanding of the God-given purpose of your own life.

OBJECTIVES. The primary objective of this book is obedience to the greatest commandment: "Thou shalt love the Lord thy God with all thy heart, and with all thy soul, and with all thy might" (Deut. 6:5, KJV). The second objective is obedience to the second greatest commandment: "Thou shalt love thy neighbor as thyself" (Matt. 22:37-40, KJV). The third objective is to secure for our nation blessings that result from obedience to God's commandments. "Blessed is the nation whose God is the LORD." (Ps. 33:11, KJV). "Righteousness exalt[s] a nation: but sin is a reproach to any people" (Prov. 14:34, KJV). "If my people, which are called by my name, shall humble themselves, and pray, and seek my face, and turn from their wicked ways; then will I hear from heaven, and will forgive their sin, and will heal their land" (2 Chron 7:14, KJV).

FOR SUCH A TIME AS THIS. The 2016 election will affect the direction of the United States for many years to come. The next president will nominate Supreme Court justices who will serve for life. The decisions of the president, Congress, and the Supreme Court will determine what laws we live under and whether we are "one nation under God." Accept this challenge and warning as from the LORD.

> And Mordecai told them to answer Esther: "Do not think in your heart that you will escape in the king's palace any more than all the other Jews. For if you remain completely silent at this time, relief and deliverance will arise for the Jews from another place, but you and your father's house will perish. Yet who knows whether you have come to the kingdom for such a time as this?" (Esther 4:13-14, NKJV)[1]

APATHY. "All that is needed for evil to triumph is for good men to do nothing."[2] The Founding Fathers founded our nation as "one nation under God." Today most Christians stand silently on the sidelines as God is removed from our schools, workplace, and government. During every national election, millions of Christians do not vote. Some do not vote because they do not like any of the candidates. By refusing to choose between the lesser of two evils, they help ensure that the most evil rule our nation.

---

[1] Holy Bible, New King James Version. Nashville: Thomas Nelson, Inc., 1982.

[2] "All that is necessary for the triumph of evil is that good men do nothing." "This is probably the most quoted statement attributed to Burke, and an extraordinary number of variants of it exist, but all without any definite original source. "Edmund Burke," Wikiquote, http://en.wikiquote.org/wiki/Edmund_Burke.

DEFINING CHRISTIAN. A Christian is not simply someone who believes in Christ or attends church. Being a Christian requires living and voting Christian values. Politics is faith in action, and every vote is a vote for or against God and the laws that He created to govern men and nations. "Faith without works is dead" (James 2:20; 2:26). On Judgment Day Christ will reject many who claim to be Christians because they failed to live Christian values. Christ said,

> Not every one that saith unto me, "Lord, Lord," shall enter into the kingdom of heaven; but he that doeth the will of my Father which is in heaven. Many will say to me in that day, "Lord, Lord, have we not prophesied in thy name? and in thy name have cast out devils? and in thy name done many wonderful works?" And then will I profess unto them, I never knew you: depart from me, ye that work iniquity (Matt. 7:21-23, KJV).

CHRISTIAN LEADERS. Christian leaders who teach that God does not care about politics, law, or government have failed God, our nation, and the people they serve. They do not fully understand God, scripture, or what being a Christian requires. Why do so many Christian leaders fail to provide moral guidance to Christians in the area of politics, law, and government? First and foremost, some mistakenly believe their first priority should be obedience to the Great Commission, saving souls for Christ. Their first priority should be obedience to the Greatest Commandment, loving God with all their heart, mind, soul, and strength. Their lives should be God-centered, not man-centered. Second, they neglect part of the Great Commission: "teaching all that I have commanded you."

9

Third, they fail to fully understand God, overemphasizing His love and neglecting His holiness, which cheapens Christ's death on the cross. Fourth, they try to be invitational, avoiding divisive issues, to welcome non-believers and to maintain peace within their congregations.

SEPARATION OF CHURCH AND STATE. Today most Americans believe in separation of church and state in a way that would be anathema to God and the founding fathers. Christians and Christian leaders who believe that God does not care about politics, law, or government or how we vote demonstrate amazing lack of understanding of God and Scripture. Many believe that God only cares about spiritual matters. They are dead wrong.

God cares more than we can possibly care about the moral state of our nation and whether we live and vote His values. First, God cares because He is the one true God, who created all the laws that govern men and nations. Second, God cares because he is love. He loves each of us more than we can possibly love ourselves. Third, God cares because He is holy. He cannot and will not in any way tolerate sin. He will judge and punish all sin. The holy, loving, God who created all things seen and unseen and the laws that govern men and nations cares more about what men and laws govern our nation than we can possibly care.

IGNORANCE. "Ignorance is not a virtue in politics or in life. It's not cool to not know what you are talking about...." Those very true words were spoken by President Obama in a commencement speech on May 21, 2016. Christ said, "Ye do err, not knowing the Scriptures, nor the power of God" (Matt. 22:28-30, KJV). During every national election, millions of Americans who call themselves Christians vote contrary to

Christian values because they do not know scripture needed to vote Christian values and to be salt and light in our schools, workplace, and government.

VOTER GUIDANCE. Christians should vote first based upon principles and laws revealed by God through scripture. They should vote second based upon principles and laws embodied in the Declaration of Independence, the Constitution, and the Bill of Rights. They should vote for candidates who support Supreme Court justices who will uphold the Constitution.

Where can Christians look for voter guidance? First, they should NOT look to their pastors or priests. They give totally conflicting guidance. They have little knowledge or understanding of Scripture related to politics, law, and government. Second, Christians can look to Christian public policy organizations for Scripture-based voter guidance. Chapters 2.1 to 2.3 review guidance from these organizations (Presidential Voter Guide, Congressional Scorecards, etc.). Third, anyone who wants a summary of the guidance that this book provides may read the Conclusion.

BOOK ORGANIZATION. This book is divided into sections and chapters. Most chapters show amazing differences between Republicans and Democrats in how they stand in relation to principles embodied in Scripture, the Declaration of Independence, the Constitution, and the Bill of Rights. Chapter 1 is the Introduction. Chapters 2.1 to 2.3 review Christian voter guidance provided by Christian organizations. Chapters 3.1 to 3.4 discuss principles of living and voting Christian values. Chapter 4.0 highlights the vital importance of voting for the Supreme Court.

Chapters 5.1 to 5.4 discuss scripture on key issues (role of government, taxes, abortion, homosexuality and same-sex marriage). Chapters 6.1 to 6.3 show what voting in accordance with the principles embodied in the Declaration of Independence, Constitution, and Bill of Rights requires. Chapters 7.1 to 7.3 discuss what voting for rights and freedoms requires (liberty, pursuit of happiness, freedom of speech and freedom of religion, and the right to bear arms). Chapters 8.1 to 8.5 address issues related to truth and character. Chapters 9.1 to 9.6 discuss other key issues (jobs, economy, national security, terrorism, immigration, healthcare, education, and climate change). Chapter 10, the Conclusion, provides a summary of the book.

CHAPTER 2.0

CHRISTIAN VOTER GUIDANCE

SECTION REVIEW. This section contains Christian voter guidance developed by Christian organizations. The first chapter list sources of Christian voter guidance. The second reviews the "2016 Values Voter Presidential Voter Guide" published by FRC Action. The third chapter discusses congressional vote scorecards developed by Family Research Council, Family Policy Alliance (formerly CitizenLink), and AFA Action. The fourth reviews congressional vote scorecards developed by National Right to Life.

CHAPTERS: Chapters in this section include the following:
  2.1 Sources of Christian Voter Guidance
  2.2 Presidential Voter Guide
  2.3 Congressional Scorecard: FRC Action and
     Family Policy Alliance (CitizenLink)
  2.4 Congressional Scorecard: National Right to Life

SOURCES OF CHRISTIAN VOTER GUIDANCE

Christians who need voter guidance may go to the websites of these Christian organizations.

FRC Action (Family Research Council Action) www.FRCaction.org. Click on Voter Resources for: (1) Voter Registration: Tool for voter registration. (2) Scorecard: Click on "Pick a Session" to see how all members of Congress voted. Note extreme difference between Republicans and Democrats. (3) State Groups: State level voter guidance.

Family Policy Alliance (formerly CitizenLink) (www.FamilyPolicyAlliance.com). Affiliate of Focus on the Family. Develops congressional scorecards with FRC Action. Click on Issues for information on Life, Family, and Religious Freedom.

American Family Association Action (www.afa.net). Click on "Get the Voter Guide" and enter state and email address to get voter registration information and voter guidance for your state.

National Right to Life (www.NRLC.org). Click on Legislation for House and Senate Scorecards which show how all members of Congress voted on life-related issues. Click on Issues for information on many life-related issues.

National Right to Life (www.NRLC.org). Click on Legislation for House and Senate Scorecards which show how all members of Congress voted on life-related issues. Click on Issues for information on many life-related issues.

Heritage Foundation (www.Heritage.org). Click on Issues for detailed written briefs on economy, federal budget, national debt, deficit, taxes, entitlements, health care, Medicare, social security, welfare, family, marriage, education, energy, environment, immigration, terrorism, and other topics.

PRESIDENTIAL VOTER GUIDE

INTRODUCTION. FRC Action published the "2016 Values Voter Presidential Voter Guide," which can be downloaded from www.FRCAction.org. It reveals sharp differences between Trump and Clinton. It shows the positions of candidates on 12 issues: marriage, abortion, Planned Parenthood, religious liberty, stem cell research, estate tax, natural marriage, ENDA/Equality Act, Obamacare, education, military, and women in combat.

ABORTION, PLANNED PARENTHOOD. Trump opposes taxpayer funding of abortions. Clinton supports it. In other words, Clinton supports using taxpayer dollars taken from Americans who believe that abortion is murder to pay for abortions. Trump opposes taxpayer funding of Planned Parenthood, the number one provider of abortions in the United States. Clinton supports taxpayer funding of Planned Parenthood.

RELIGIOUS LIBERTY. Trump supports legislation that protects Christians from "government discrimination" regarding marriage, abortion, and sexuality. Amazingly, Clinton actually opposes legislation to protect Christians from discrimination.

OBAMACARE. Trump supports repeal of Obamacare, which forces all Americans to purchase health care insurance or pay a hefty fine. Clinton opposes repeal of Obamacare.

EDUCATION. Trump supports legislation that protects the rights of parents to make choices regarding what private and public schools their children attend. Clinton opposes it.

ESTATE TAX. Trump supports repeal of the federal estate tax, which robs children of their inheritance from their parents. Clinton opposes repeal of the federal estate tax.

MARRIAGE, NATURAL MARRIAGE. Clinton supports the Supreme Court decision that made same-sex marriage legal. Trump's position is unknown. Both oppose an amendment to the U.S. Constitution that defines marriage as "the union of one man and one woman."

STEM CELL RESEARCH. Clinton supports federal funding o f "embryo-destructive stem cell research. Trump's position is unknown.

ENDA/EQUALITY ACT. Clinton supports legislation that creates "special protections" for LGBT (Lesbian Gay Bisexual Transvestite) personnel. Trumps position is unknown.

MILITARY; WOMEN IN DRAFT. Clinton opposes any efforts to repeal social policies that President Obama imposed upon the military that granted special protections based upon sexual orientation and placement o f women in frontline combat units. Trump's positions are mixed. The positions of Trump and Clinton on including women in the draft are unknown.

CONCLUSION. The 2016 Presidential Values Voter Presidential Guide shows that Clinton opposes Christian values on 11 of 12 issues, and her position is unknown on one issue.

Trump supports Christian values on 6 of 12 issues. His positions are unknown on 4 issues and mixed on one. He is wrong on only one position.

CONGRESSIONAL SCORECARD: FRC ACTION AND FAMILY POLICY ALLIANCE (CITIZENLINK)

INTRODUCTION. The best way to evaluate a candidate is not to look at what he said or promised when trying to get elected, but how he actually voted. Voting records reveal extreme differences between Republicans and Democrats. Most Republicans vote Christian values most of the time. Most Democrats vote against Christian values most of the time. The extreme degree to which this is true is almost beyond belief, but clearly proven by scorecards that show exactly how elected officials voted on issues that required the application of Christian values. The conclusion to this chapter provides a very detailed summary of the results of these scorecards, for those who do not wish to read the all the details regarding all the votes.

Each year Family Research Council Action (FRC Action) and Family Policy Alliance, an affiliate of Focus on the Family (formerly called Citizenlink) or American Family Association Action (AFA Action) produce a "Vote Scorecard" that shows how members of Congress voted on "the most clear-cut, pro-family votes." This chapter will review the scorecards published during two election years: 2008 and 2012. During 2008, FRC Action and CitizenLink published a scorecard for 100th Congress, First Session that covered votes cast during 2007.[3] During 2012, FRC Action and CitizenLink

---

[3] FRC Action and Focus on the Family Action, "Vote Scorecard, 110th Congress, 1st Session," http://www.frcaction.org (accessed July 9, 2008).

published a scorecard for 112th Congress, First Session that covered votes cast during 2011.[4] Go to http://www.frcaction.org to view scorecards and see exactly how every member of Congress voted.

2008 SENATE SCORECARD. The 2008 scorecard reveals extreme disparity between the voting records of Republicans and Democrats in the U.S. Senate. **Senator Clinton, Senator Obama, and Senator Biden scored 0%.** Republicans scored an amazingly high average of 86%. Most Republicans scored 100% (58%; 29 of 50). They voted with Christian values, with FRC Action and CitizenLink, on all 7 issues. Ten Republicans (20%) scored 85-99%. Seven Republicans (14%) scored 57-71%. One Republican (2%) scored 42% (Senator McCain). Three Republicans (6%) scored 28% (Senators Collins and Snowe of Connecticut and Spector of Pennsylvania). No Republican scored lower than 28%. Democrats scored an average of only 8.02%, less than one-tenth the average score of Republicans.[5]

Most Democrats scored 0% (67%; 33 of 49). They voted against Christian values, against the positions of FRC Action and CitizenLink, on all 7 issues. Eleven Democrats (22%) scored 14%. One Democrat (2%) scored 28%. Three Democrats (6%) scored 42%. One Democrat (2%) scored 85% (Senator Nelson of Nebraska). No Democrat scored 100%.[6]

Senators were evaluated on 7 critical "pro-family" issues. The legislation included:

---

[4] FRC Action and Citizenlink, "Vote Scorecard, 112th Congress, 1st Session," http://www.frcaction.org (accessed February 17, 2012).
[5] FRC Action and Focus on the Family Action, "Vote Scorecard, 110th Congress, 1st Session," http://www.frcaction.org (accessed July 9, 2008).
[6] Ibid.

Issue 1: An amendment to the Lobby Reform Act to protect grassroots organizations from unfair regulation of lobbying activities;[7]

Issue 2: The Embryonic Stem Cell Research Act, a bill funding embryonic stem cell research that required destruction of human embryos;[8]

Issue 3: An amendment to the State Children's Health Insurance Program to allow states to provide health insurance for unborn children;[9]

Issue 4: An amendment to the State, Foreign Operations and Related Programs Appropriations Act to prevent funding of international groups "that support or participate in coercive abortion or involuntary sterilization programs;"[10]

Issue 5: An amendment to the same Act that would have funded international organizations "that perform and promote abortions as a method of family planning;[11]

Issue 6: A "thought crimes amendment" to the Department of Defense Authorization that "would establish federal 'hate crimes' for certain violent acts based on the actual or perceived race, religion, disability, gender identity or sexual orientation of any person;"[12] and

Issue 7: Confirmation of Judge Southwick, nominated by President Bush, to the U.S. Court of Appeals.[13]

Senate Republicans sponsored all 4 bills, amendments or motions supporting Christian values. No Democrat sponsored any pro-Christian, pro-family values legislation, but

---

[7] Ibid.
[8] Ibid.
[9] Ibid.
[10] Ibid.
[11] Ibid.
[12] Ibid.
[13] Ibid.

they did sponsor 3 bills or amendments contrary to Christian values. Most Senate Democrats supported all anti-Christian legislation opposed by Republicans (Issues 1,2,4,5,6). They opposed all pro-Christian values legislation supported by Republicans (Issue 3) and opposed confirmation of conservative federal judge who supports Christian values (Issue 7).

Most Senate Republicans opposed: (1) laws regulating lobbying that inhibit Christian organizations from providing information to the public on matters before Congress (Issue 1); (2) federal funds for embryonic stem cell research that require destruction of human embryos (Issue 2); (3) federal funds for international groups that support abortion or involuntary sterilization (Issues 4,5); (4) hate crimes laws that wrongfully criminalize thoughts not just actions regarding "race, religion, disability, gender identity or sexual orientation" (Issue 6). Most Republicans supported: (1) confirmation of a federal judge who supports Christian values (Issue 7) and (2) laws that permit states to have health insurance for unborn children (Issue 3).

2008 HOUSE OF REPRESENTATIVES SCORECARD. The 2008 scorecard also reveals extreme disparity between the voting records of Republicans and Democrats in the U.S. House of Representatives. Republicans scored an average of 87%. Congressman Pence scored 93% (100% in 2012). Most Republicans scored 100% (53%; 108 of 203). They voted Christian values, with the positions of FRC Action and CitizenLink, on all 11 issues. 54 Republicans (27%) scored 76-99%. 26 Republicans (13%) scored 51-75%. Nine Republicans (4.4%) scored 26-50%. Five Republicans (2%) scored 1-25% (Congressman Shays of Connecticut, Castle of Delaware, Kirk of Illinois, Gilchrest of Maryland,

and Frelinghuysen of New Jersey). Only one Republican (0.5 %) scored 0% (Congressman Norwood of Georgia).[14]

Democrats scored an average of only 10%, about one-eighth the average score of Republicans. Almost half of the Democrats scored 0% (46%; 109 of 235). They always voted against Christian values, against the positions of FRC Action and CitizenLink. 72 Democrats (another 31%) scored only 6%, barely above 0. 29 Democrats (12%) scored 12-25%. 9 Democrats (4%) scored 26-50%. 9 Democrats (4%) scored 51-75%. Only 5 of 235 Democrats (2%) scored 76-99% (Congressman Marshall of Georgia, Ellsworth of Indiana, Peterson of Minnesota, and Taylor of Mississippi Lincoln Davis of Tennessee. Only 2 of 235 Democrats (1%) scored 100% (Congressmen McIntyre and Shuler of North Carolina).[15]

Representatives were evaluated on 16 "pro-family" issues. The legislation included:

Issue 1: A motion to recommit the Embryonic Stem Cell Research Act that would ensure that taxpayer funds were not used for human cloning."[16]

Issue 2: The Embryonic Stem Cell Research Act, which would fund stem cell research that required destruction of human embryos.[17]

Issue 3: A motion to recommit the Head Start Reauthorization bill that would remove a provision that "prevents faith-based organizations from hiring according to their faith.[18]

---

[14] Ibid.
[15] Ibid.
[16] Ibid.
[17] Ibid.
[18] Ibid.

Issue 4: Federal Hate Crimes Act, a "thought crimes bill" that "would establish federal 'hate crimes' for certain violent acts based on the actual or perceived race, religion, disability, gender identity or sexual orientation of any person."[19]

Issue 5: Human Cloning Protection Act, a bill that would allow "the creation of cloned human embryos for destructive research."[20]

Issue 6: Embryonic Stem Cell Research Act, a bill funding embryonic stem cell research that required destruction of human embryos.[21]

Issue 7: An amendment to the State, Foreign Operations and Related Programs Appropriations Act that would require "a third of HIV/AIDs prevention funding to be spent for 'abstinence-until-marriage' and 'be-faithful' programs.[22]

Issue 8: A amendment to the State, Foreign Operations and Related Programs Appropriations Act that would allow "taxpayer funded contraceptives to be given to international organizations that perform and promote abortions as a method of family planning."[23]

Issue 9: An amendment to same Act that would have "upheld the prohibition against federal funding of international organizations that perform and promote abortions as a method of family planning."[24]

Issue 10: State, Foreign Operations and Related Programs Appropriations Act, a bill that undermines the funding of "abstinence-until-marriage" and "be-faithful"

---

[19] Ibid.
[20] Ibid.
[21] Ibid.
[22] Ibid.
[23] Ibid.
[24] Ibid.

programs and the prohibition of federal funding of "international organizations that perform or promote abortions as a method of family planning."[25]

Issue 11: An amendment to the Financial Services and General Government Appropriations Act that restricts funding of needle exchange programs in the District of Columbia.[26]

Issue 12: An amendment to the same Act that "strips the Federal Communications Commission of the authority to reinstitute" the..."Fairness Doctrine"...that would "order broadcasters to give equal air time to both sides of controversial issues."[27]

Issue 13: Another amendment to the same Act that would prevent federal funds from being used by the District of Columbia for domestic partner benefits.[28]

Issue 14: An amendment to the Labor, Health and Human Services and Education Appropriations Act that would restrict use of federal funds for abortions by withholding $331 million appropriated to Planned Parenthood, the nation's leading abortion provider, for "family planning services."[29]

Issue 15: The Children's Health and Medicine Protection Act, a bill that reauthorizes and expands the State Children's Health Insurance Program. It undermines health coverage for unborn children, allows states to provide family planning services for individuals not eligible for Medicaid, and undermine abstinence education.[30]

Issue 16: The Employment Non-Discrimination Act, it provides special protection for homosexuals not given to other

---

[25] Ibid.
[26] Ibid.
[27] Ibid.
[28] Ibid.
[29] Ibid.
[30] Ibid.

employees and radically transforms workplace discrimination law.[31]

In the House of Representatives, Republicans sponsored 7 pro-family, pro-Christian bills, amendments, or motions, and Democrats sponsored 8 contrary to Christian values. A Republican and a Democrat jointly sponsored only 1 of the 16 issues. Most Democrats in the House supported all anti-Christian values legislation supported by Republicans and opposed all pro-Christian values legislation supported by Republicans.

Most Republicans in the House, like Republicans in the Senate, opposed: (1) federal funds for embryonic stem cell research that requires the destruction of human embryos (Issues 2,6); (2) federal funds for groups that support abortion (Issues 8,9,10); (3) hate crimes laws which wrongfully criminalize thoughts not just actions regarding "race, religion, disability, gender identity or sexual orientation" (Issue 4). House Republicans also opposed: (1) use of taxpayer funds for cloning human embryos for destructive research (Issues 1,5); (2) legislation that prevents faith-based organizations from hiring according to their faith for the Head Start Program (Issue 3); (3) a law which would require part of HIV/AIDs prevention funding to be spent for "abstinence-until-marriage" and "be-faithful" programs (Issues 7,10); (4) restrictions on funds for needle exchange programs in the District of Columbia (Issue 11); (5) the 'Fairness Doctrine,' which would inhibit Christian broadcasters by forcing them to give equal time to both sides of issues (Issue 12); (6) use of federal funds by the District of Columbia for domestic partner benefits (Issue 13); (7) use of federal funds for abortions by Planned Parenthood (Issue 14); (8) allowing states to fund family

---

[31] Ibid.

planning for those not eligible for Medicaid and requiring states to fund family planning as part of Medicaid (Issue 15); (9) granting special consideration on the basis of "sexual orientation" not extended to other employees in the workplace (Issue 16). House Republicans supported state health coverage for unborn children and state abstinence education programs (Issue 15).

2012 SENATE SCORECARD. The 2012 scorecard reveals extreme disparity between the voting records of Republicans and Democrats in the U.S. Senate. The average score for Republicans was 73%. The average score for Democrats was less than 2% (1.65%). No Democrat scored above 14%. 88% of Democrats scored an absolute 0%.[32]

Senators were evaluated on 7 "pro-family" issues. The legislation included:

Issue 1: An amendment to the FAA Authorization Bill that would repeal Obamacare, the national health care law called the Patient Protection and Affordable Care Act, a law that funded abortion, denied conscience protections, and instituted health care rationing.[33]

Issue 2: A Continuing Resolution to fund abortion in the District of Columbia that did not exclude funding for Planned Parenthood.[34]

Issue 3: An amendment to the Department of Defense and Full Year Continuing Appropriations Act of 2011 that would prevent funding of the health care act (Patient Protection and Affordable Care Act), a law that funded

---

[32] FRC Action and Citizenlink, "Vote Scorecard, 112th Congress, 1st Session," http://www.frcaction.org (accessed February 17, 2012).
[33] Ibid.
[34] Ibid.

abortion, denied conscience protections, and instituted health care rationing.[35]

Issue 4: An amendment to the Department of Defense and Full Year Continuing Appropriations Act of 2011 that would prevent funding of Planned Parenthood, the nation's largest abortion provider.[36]

Issue 5: A vote on John McConnell for U.S. District Judge. Nominated by President Obama, there was evidence that he would not be an impartial judge and that he would legislate from the bench.[37]

Issue 6: A vote on Goodwin Liu for U.S. Court of Appeals Circuit Judge. Nominated by President Obama, there was evidence that he would be an activist judge and replace the Constitution with personal views.[38]

Issue 7: A bill that would authorize the President to make appointments to thousands of government positions without Senate confirmation.[39]

2012 HOUSE OF REPRESENTATIVES SCORECARD. The 2012 scorecard also reveals extreme disparity between the voting records of Republicans and Democrats in the U.S. House of Representatives. The average score for Republicans was about 89%. The average score for Democrats was about 9%. 91% of Democrats scored 10% or less.[40] Congressman Pence, a Republican, scored 100%.

Representatives were evaluated on 10 "pro-family" issues. The legislation included:

---

[35] Ibid.

[36] Ibid.

[37] Ibid.

[38] Ibid.

[39] Ibid.

[40] Ibid.

Issue 1: The Repealing the Job-Killing Health Care Law would repeal Obamacare, the national health care law called the Patient Protection and Affordable Care Act, a law that funded abortion, denied conscience protections, and instituted health care rationing.[41]

Issue 2: An amendment to the Full-Year Continuing Appropriations Act that would prevent funding of Planned Parenthood, the nation's largest abortion provider.[42]

Issue 3: A Continuing Resolution with funding for abortion in the District of Columbia and funding for Planned Parenthood.[43]

Issue 4: The Scholarships for Opportunity and Results Act would reauthorize the D.C. Opportunity Scholarship Program to allow students in the District of Columbia to attend the school of their choice.[44]

Issue 5: An amendment to the Department of Defense and Full Year Continuing Appropriations Act of 2011 that would prevent funding of Obamacare, the national health care law called the Patient Protection and Affordable Care Act, a law that funded abortion, denied conscience protections, and instituted health care rationing.[45]

Issue 6: An amendment to the Department of Defense and Full Year Continuing Appropriations Act of 2011 that would prevent funding of Planned Parenthood, the nation's largest abortion provider.[46]

Issue 7: The No Taxpayer Funding of Abortion Act was an amendment that would permanently prevent federal funds from paying for abortions and health care plans that

---

[41] Ibid.
[42] Ibid.
[43] Ibid.
[44] Ibid.
[45] Ibid.
[46] Ibid.

covered abortions and protect conscience rights of health care providers who objected to doing abortions.[47]

Issue 8: The Foxx amendment to change Obamacare, the national health care law called the Patient Protection and Affordable Care Act, to bar federal funding of abortions and use for educating medical students on how to perform abortions.[48]

Issue 9: An amendment to the Department of Defense Appropriations Act of 2012 that would prevent Pentagon funds from being used contrary to Defense of Marriage Act.[49]

Issue 10: Another amendment to the same Act that would prohibit funding of Navy a directive allowing chaplains to perform same-sex marriages in violation of the Defense of Marriage Act.[50]

CONCLUSION. The scorecards jointly produced by Family Research Council Action (FRC Action) and Citizenlink, an affiliate of Focus on the Family, show how members of Congress voted on "the most clear-cut, pro-family votes." The 2008 Senate scorecard showed that Senator Clinton, Senator Obama, and Senator Biden scored 0%. Trump did not serve in Congress, so he is not on the scorecards. Senate Republicans scored an average of 86%. Most Republicans scored 100% (58%; 29 of 50). Senate Democrats scored an average of only 8.02%, less than one-tenth the average score of Republicans. Most Democrats scored 0% (67%; 33 of 49).

In the House of Representatives, Republicans scored an average of 87%. Most Republicans scored 100% (53%; 108 of

---

[47] Ibid.
[48] Ibid.
[49] Ibid.
[50] Ibid.

203). Congressman Pence scored 93% (100% in 2012). Democrats scored an average of only 10%, about one-eighth the average score of Republicans. Almost half of the Democrats scored 0% (46%; 109 of 235). 72 Democrats (another 31%) scored only 6%, barely above 0. In other words, 77% of Democrats (181 if 235) scored either 0% or 6%.

On the 2012 Senate scorecard, the average score for Republicans was 73%. The average score for Democrats was less than 2% (1.65%). No Democrat scored above 14%. 88% of Democrats scored an absolute 0%. In the House of Representatives, the average score for Republicans was about 89%. The average score for Democrats was about 9%. 91% of Democrats scored 10% or less.

Knowing these facts raises a couple questions. How can anyone who calls himself a Christian vote for any Democrat knowing that Democrats are so united in voting against Christian values? How can any Christian do anything that would help put Democrats in power, knowing that they would govern totally contrary to simple, basic moral laws revealed by God through Scripture? Jesus said His food was to do the will of His Father. Voting for a Democrat or doing anything that would put Democrats in power is totally contrary to what it means to be a Christian.

CHAPTER 2.4

CONGRESSIONAL SCORECARD:
NATIONAL RIGHT TO LIFE

INTRODUCTION. National Right to Life produces "Vote Scorecards" similar to that of Family Research Council Action and Citizenlink (formerly Focus Action). They show how members of Congress voted on issues related to abortion, health care, etc. All voting results discussed within this chapter are from the National Right to Life Committee (NRLC) "Federal NRLC Scorecard" for 110th Congress and 112th Congress.[51] The author of this book calculated all percentages. Go to http://www.nrlc.org to view scorecards and see exactly how every member of Congress voted. The conclusion to this chapter provides a very detailed summary of the results of these scorecards, for those who do not wish to read the all the details regarding all the votes.

2008 SENATE SCORECARD. The 2008 National Right to Life scorecard for 110th Congress reveals amazing disparity between the voting records of Republicans and Democrats in the U.S. Senate. **Senator Clinton, Senator Obama, and Senator Biden scored 0%.** Senate Republicans scored an average of 88%. Most Republicans scored 100% (63%; 32 of 51). Eleven Republicans (22%) scored 83-85%. Five Republicans (10%) scored 57-66%. Three Republicans

---

[51] National Right to Life Committee, "Federal NRLC Scorecard - 110th Congress, Combined Sessions," http://www.nrlc.org (accessed July 7, 2008); National Right to Life Committee, "Federal NRLC Scorecard - 110th Congress, Combined Sessions," http://www.nrlc.org (accessed July 21, 2012).

(6%) scored only 14%. No Republican scored lower.[52]

In 2008 Senate Democrats scored an average of only 9%, about one-tenth the average score of Republicans. Most Democrats scored 0% (71%; 35 of 49). They voted against the position of NRLC, against Christian values, on all 7 issues. Six Democrats (12%) scored 14%. Five Democrats (10%) scored 28-33%. Two Democrats (4%) scored 57-66%. One Democrat (2%) scored 85% (Senator Nelson of Nebraska). No Democrat scored 100%.[53]

Senators were evaluated on 7 critical "pro-family" issues. The legislation included:

Issue 1: Regulation of "grassroots lobbying" groups. Amendment (No. 20) to 2007 Lobby Reform Act (S.1) This amendment "infringed on rights protected by the First Amendment, and would inhibit groups from providing timely motivating information to members of the public about matters under consideration in Congress." It would "require registration and reporting by certain activists and groups who spend money to encourage members of the general public to communicate with members of Congress or other federal officials about legislative and policy matters." Violations would were punishable by fines of up to $200,000 and prison terms of up to 10 years.[54]

Issue 2: Stem Cell Research Enhancement Act (S. 5). This bill "would mandate federal funding of the type of stem cell research that requires the killing of human embryos."[55]

---

[52] National Right to Life Committee, "Federal NRLC Scorecard - 110th Congress, Combined Sessions," http://www.nrlc.org (accessed July 7, 2008).
[53] Ibid.
[54] Ibid.
[55] Ibid.

Issue 3: Medicare prescription drug price controls (Senate Bill 3). This bill would prevent "older people from being allowed to spend their own money...to save their own lives through access to unrationed prescription drugs under Medicare. Under the guise of allowing "government negotiation" the bill would authorize the imposition of price controls that would limit access to and discourage the development of innovative life-saving medicines."[56]

Issue 4: Health Insurance for Unborn Child. Amendment (No. 2535) to H.R. 976, a bill to reauthorize the State Children's Health Insurance Program (SCHIP). "The State Children's Health Insurance (SCHIP) program is a federal program that provides funds to states primarily to provide health services to children of low-income families. The Amendment states that a covered child "includes, at the option of a State, an unborn child."[57]

Issue 5: Banning Funding of Organizations that Support Coercive Abortion Programs. Amendment (No. 2707) to the Senate State, Foreign Operations and Related Programs Appropriations Act 2008 (H.R. 2764). The Kemp-Kasten Anti-Coercion law has been in effect since 1985. It prohibits U.S. "population assistance" funds from going to any organization that "supports or participates in the management of a program of coercive abortion or involuntary sterilization." "However, in crafting the Fiscal Year 2008 State-Foreign Operations Appropriations Bill (H.R. 2764), the Senate Appropriations Committee removed the traditional Kemp-Kasten language.... Senator Sam Brownback (R-Ks.) offered an NRLC-backed amendment...to restore the...Kemp-Kasten anti-coercion language."[58]

Issue 6: Funding International Abortion Groups.

---

[56] Ibid.
[57] Ibid.
[58] Ibid.

Amendment (No. 2719) to the Senate State, Foreign Operations and Related Programs Appropriations Act 2008 (H.R. 2764). "Known as the "Boxer Amendment to overturn pro-life "Mexico City Policy"... Under the pro-life "Mexico City Policy," private overseas organizations that "perform or actively promote abortion as a method of family planning" are not eligible to receive funds for "population assistance." Pro-abortion Senator Boxer (D-Ca.) offered an amendment to prohibit enforcement of any pro-life policy.[59]

Issue 7: Prohibition on Abortion Services in Indian Health Programs. Vitter amendment to Senate Bill 1200. The federal government funds health programs for American Indians. During the 1970s, it paid for abortions. Funding of abortions was stopped in the 1980s, but this policy depended on annual renewal of the Hyde Amendment. On February 26, 2008, , Senator Vitter (R-La.) offered an NRLC-backed amendment to permanently prohibit coverage of abortion (except to save the life of the mother, or in cases of rape or incest)."[60]

Note the types of legislation supported by Republicans and Democrats in the Senate. Most Republicans opposed: (1) laws regulating lobbying that would inhibit Christian organizations from providing information to the public on matters before Congress (Senate issue 1); (2) federal funds for embryonic stem cell research that require the destruction of human embryos (Senate issue 2); (3) laws that would impose "price controls that would limit access to and discourage the development of innovative life-saving medicines" for elderly Americans using Medicare (Senate Issue 3); (4) federal funds for international groups that support abortion or involuntary sterilization (Senate issue 5,6);and (5) federal funds for

---

[59] Ibid.
[60] Ibid.

abortions by American Indians (Senate issue7). Most Republicans supported: (1) laws that permit states to have health insurance for unborn children (Senate issue 4). Most Senate Democrats supported all anti-Christian legislation opposed by Republicans and opposed all pro-Christian values legislation supported by Republicans.

     2008 HOUSE OF REPRESENTATIVES SCORECARD. The 2008 National Right to Life Committee (NRLC) Scorecard also reveals great disparity between the voting records of Republicans and Democrats in the U.S. House of Representatives. House Republicans scored an average of 88%. A large majority of Republicans scored 100% (71%; 143 of 201). They voted on all 7 pro-family issues, and they always voted with the recommendation of NRLC. 20 Republicans (10%) scored 76-99%. 19 Republicans (9.5%) scored 51-75%. 11 Republicans (5.5%) scored 26-50%. Five Republicans (2.5%) scored 1-25%). Three Republicans (0.5 %) scored 0%.[61]

     In 2008 House Democrats scored an average of only 7%, less than one-tenth the average score of Republicans. A very large majority of Democrats scored 0% (85%; 199 of 233). They always voted against the position of NRLC, against Christian values, on all issues. 10 Democrats (4%) scored 1-25%. 8 Democrats (3%) scored 26-50%. 8 Democrats (3%) scored 51-75%. 8 Democrats (3%) scored 76-99%. No Democrat scored 100%.[62]

     Representatives were evaluated on 7 critical "pro-family" issues. The legislation included:
     Issue 1: Prohibition on Funding of Human Cloning.

---

[61] Ibid.
[62] Ibid.

Stem Cell Research Enhancement Act" (H.R. 3) Anti-Cloning Amendment. "On January 11, 2007, the House of Representatives debated H.R. 3, authored by Rep. Diana DeGette (D-Co.) and Mike Castle (R-De.), a bill that would mandate federal funding of the type of stem cell research that requires the killing of human embryos in order to harvest their stem cells. The embryos would be those "donated from in vitro fertilization clinics, [and that] were created for the purposes of fertility treatment," after authorization by the parents. The bill, which NRLC strongly opposed, is intended to overturn the pro-life policy that President Bush announced on August 9, 2001, under which federal funds do not support research that requires the killing of human embryos. The House Democratic leadership brought the bill to the floor under a "closed rule," which allowed the pro-life side to offer only a single proposed modification to the bill. This amendment (technically called a "motion to recommit with instructions") would have added language to the bill to prohibit any of the funds authorized by the bill from being given to labs or other entities that do research on stem cells obtained from human embryos created by cloning. NRLC is opposed to human cloning, so NRLC supported this anti-human-cloning motion/amendment."[63]

Issue 2: Stem Cell Research. Embryonic Stem Cell Research Enhancement Act (H.R. 3). H.R. 3 was "a bill that would mandate federal funding of the type of stem cell research that requires the killing of human embryos in order to harvest their stem cells."[64]

Issue 3: Medicare Prescription Drug Price Negotiation Act (H.R. 4). This bill "would effectively prevent older people from being allowed to spend their own money, if they choose, to save their own lives through access to unrationed prescription drugs under Medicare. Under the guise of

---

[63] Ibid.
[64] Ibid.

"government negotiation" the bill would result in the imposition of price controls that would limit access to and discourage the development of innovative life-saving medicines."[65]

Issue 4: Phony Ban on Human Cloning. Human Cloning Protection Act (H.R. 2560). This bill (H.R. 2560) is "deceptively titled "The Human Cloning Prohibition Act." But in reality H.R. 2560 does not ban any human cloning at all. H.R. 2560 would allow the creation of any number of cloned human embryos, for the specific purpose of harvesting their stem cells or using them in other research that will kill them. H.R. 2560 actually bans only allowing a human clone to live, by implanting her or him "into a uterus or the functional equivalent of a uterus," or "to ship, mail, transport, or receive" such an embryo. NRLC strongly opposes this "clone-and-kill bill."[66]

Issue 5: Embryonic Stem Cell Research Enhancement Act of 2007 (S. 5). This bill "would mandate federal funding of the type of stem cell research that requires the killing of human embryos. This bill would overturn President Bush's policy that prohibits such funding."[67]

Issue 6: International Abortion Funding. Amendment (H.AMDT. 368) to the State, Foreign Operations and Related Programs Appropriations Act, 2008 (H.R. 2764). This amendment was known as the "Smith-Stupak Amendment" to protect the pro-life "Mexico City Policy." "Under President Bush's pro-life "Mexico City Policy," private overseas organizations that "perform or actively promote abortion as a method of family planning" are not eligible to receive funds under the U.S. foreign aid program for "population assistance." The Fiscal Year 2008 State-Foreign Operations Appropriations

---

[65] Ibid.
[66] Ibid.
[67] Ibid.

Bill (H.R. 2764) contained language, authored by pro-abortion Rep. Nita Lowey (D-NY), designed to undermine the "Mexico City Policy" by requiring the U.S. Agency for International Development (USAID) to provide such pro-abortion organizations with certain U.S.-funded contraceptive supplies. Pro-life Representatives Chris Smith (R-NJ) and Bart Stupak (D-Mi.) offered an amendment, which was strongly supported by NRLC, to remove the pro-abortion language from the bill."[68]

Issue 7: Restrict Funding to Planned Parenthood. Amendment (H.AMDT. 594) to the Labor, Health and Human Services, and Education Appropriations Act, 2008 (H.R. 3043). This amendment would deny federal "family-planning" funds to Planned Parenthood. "Title X ("Title 10") of the Public Health Service Act provides more than $300 million annually for grants to state and private entities for "family planning" programs. Although federal law does not permit such funds to be used to pay for abortions, large amounts of Title X funds go to organizations that operate abortion clinics, including affiliates of the Planned Parenthood Federation of America (PPFA), the nation's largest abortion provider. On July 19, 2007, during consideration of the Fiscal Year 2008 appropriations bill for the federal Department of Health and Human Services, pro-life Congressman Mike Pence (R-In.) offered an amendment to prohibit any Title X funds from going to any arm of Planned Parenthood."[69]

Note that most Republicans in the House, like Republicans in the Senate, opposed: (1) federal funds for embryonic stem cell research that requires the destruction of human embryos (House issues 2,4,5); (2) laws that would impose "price controls that would limit access to and

---

[68] Ibid.
[69] Ibid.

discourage the development of innovative life-saving medicines" for elderly Americans using Medicare (House Issue 3); (3) federal funds for international groups that support abortion or involuntary sterilization (House issue 6). House Republicans also opposed: (1) taxpayer funds for cloning human embryos for destructive research (House issue 1) and (2) federal funds for Planned Parenthood, the nation's largest abortion provider (House issue 7). Most Democrats in the House supported all anti-Christian values legislation supported by Republicans and opposed all pro-Christian values legislation supported by Republicans. No Democrat sponsored any pro-Christian, pro-life legislation, but they did sponsor all bills and amendments contrary to Christian values. Republicans sponsored all bills and amendments that support Christian values.

2012 SENATE SCORECARD. The 2012 National Right to Life Committee (NRLC) Scorecard reveals great disparity between the voting records of Republicans and Democrats in the U.S. Senate. Senators were evaluated on 5 issues. Senate Republicans scored an average of 97%. Most Republicans scored 100% (90%; 43 of 48). Only five Republicans (10%; 5 of 48) scored less than 100%. Senate Democrats scored an average of only 1%. Most Democrats scored 0% (94%; 48 of 51). They voted against the position of NRLC, against Christian values, on all issues. Only 3 Democrats (6%) scored higher than 0%.[70]

Senators were evaluated on 5 critical "pro-family" issues. The legislation included:
Issue 1: Repeal Obamacare health care law. This was

---

[70] National Right to Life Committee, "Federal NRLC Scorecard - 110th Congress, Combined Sessions," http://www.nrlc.org (accessed July 21, 2012).

an amendment to completely repeal Obamacare, the Patient Protection and Affordable Care Act, the "massive health care restructuring law enacted March 2010. The PPACA contained many provisions that would implement government –imposed rationing of life-saving health care and included federal funding of abortion.[71]

Issue 2: Block funding of Obamacare health care law. This bill was an attempt to block funding of Obamacare, the Patient Protection and Affordable Care Act discussed above.[72]

Issue 3: Cut federal funding of Planned Parenthood. This was a bill to cut all federal funding to Planned Parenthood Federation of American (PPFA), the nation's number one provider of abortions.[73]

Issue 4: Prevent Obama abortion mandates. This bill, the Respect for Rights of Conscience Act, would amend the Obamacare law to permit employers and health insurers to refuse to cover services to which they had a moral or religious objection, services such as abortion.[74]

Issue 5: "Disclose Act" to restrict political free speech. This bill, opposed by NRLC, was designed to restrict freedom of "political speech about members of Congress, candidates for Congress, and ongoing developments in Congress."[75]

2012 HOUSE OF REPRESENTATIVES SCORECARD. The 2012 National Right to Life Committee (NRLC) Scorecard reveals great disparity between the voting records of Republicans and Democrats in the House of Representatives. Members of the House of Representatives were evaluated on 5 issues. House Republicans scored an

---

[71] Ibid.
[72] Ibid.
[73] Ibid.
[74] Ibid.
[75] Ibid.

average of 98%. Most Republicans scored 100% (94%; 229 of 243). Only 14 Republicans (6%; 14 of 243) scored less than 100%. House Democrats scored an average of only 5%. Most Democrats scored 0% (88%; 171 of 194). They voted against the position of NRLC, against Christian values, on all issues. Only 23 Democrats (12%) scored higher than 0% (23 of 243).[76]

Representatives were evaluated on 9 critical "pro-family" issues. The legislation included:

Issue 1: H.R.2 to repeal Obamacare health care law. This was an amendment to completely repeal Obamacare, the Patient Protection and Affordable Care Act, the "massive health care restructuring law enacted March 2010. The PPACA contained many provisions that would implement government –imposed rationing of life-saving health care and included federal funding of abortion.[77]

Issue 2: Cut federal funding of Planned Parenthood. This was a bill to cut all federal funding to Planned Parenthood Federation of American (PPFA), the nation's number one provider of abortions.[78]

Issue 3: Block funding of Obamacare health care law. This was an amendment to block funding of the Patient Protection and Affordable Care Act, the "massive health care restructuring law enacted March 2010. The PPACA contained many provisions that would implement government –imposed rationing of life-saving health care and included federal funding of abortion.[79]

Issue 4: Cut federal funding of Planned Parenthood. This was a bill to cut all federal funding to Planned Parenthood

---

[76] Ibid.
[77] Ibid.
[78] Ibid.
[79] Ibid.

Federation of American (PPFA), the nation's number one provider of abortions.[80]

Issue 5: The No Taxpayer Funding of Abortion Act (H.R.3) would permanently block the use of federal funds for abortion and health insurance coverage of abortions by federal programs.[81]

Issue 6: This amendment would block the use of federal funds to train abortionists. It would also establish conscience protections that would prohibit any medical facility to discriminate against any doctor, nurse, or medial provider who refused to "provide, pay for, provide coverage of, or refer for abortions"[82]

Issue 7: The Protect Life Act would "repeal and/or correct all of the pro-abortion components" of Obamacare, the Patient Protection and Affordable Care Act, the "massive health care restructuring law.[83]

Issue 8: The Prenatal Nondiscrimination Act is a ban on sex-selection abortions. This law would make it illegal to knowingly: (1) perform an abortion based upon sex of child, (2) to use force or threats to coerce sex-based abortion, (3) to "solicit or accept funds" for sex-based abortions, and (4) to transport a woman across state lines or into the nation for sex-based abortion.[84]

Issue 9: Repeal of Obamacare health care law. This was an amendment to completely repeal Obamacare, the Patient Protection and Affordable Care Act, the "massive health care restructuring law enacted March 2010. The PPACA contained many provisions that would implement government –imposed rationing of life-saving health care and included federal

---

[80] Ibid.
[81] Ibid.
[82] Ibid.
[83] Ibid.
[84] Ibid.

funding of abortion.[85]

CONCLUSION. The 2008 National Right to Life Committee (NRLC) "Vote Scorecard", like the Focus Action and Family Research Council Action "Vote Scorecard", reveals extreme differences between the voting records of Republicans and Democrats. Senator Clinton and Senator Obama scored 0% for voting Christian values. Trump did not serve in Congress, so he is not on the scorecards. Most Republicans scored 100% (63%; 32 of 51), voting Christian values every time that they voted on the right to life issues selected by NRLC. Most Democrats scored 0%. Republicans scored an average of 88%. Democrats scored an average of only 9%, about one-tenth the average score of Republicans. Most Democrats scored 0% (71%; 35 of 49), always voting against Christian values.

In the U.S. House of Representatives, Republicans scored an average of 88%. Congressman Pence scored 100%. Most Republicans scored 100% (71%; 143 of 201), always voting for Christian values. Democrats scored an average of only 7%, less than one-tenth the average score of Republicans. Most Democrats scored 0% (85%; 199 of 233), voting against Christian values every time that they voted.

The 2012 National Right to Life Committee (NRLC) Scorecard reveals the same great disparity between the voting records of Republicans and Democrats. Senate Republicans scored an average of 97%. Most Republicans scored 100% (90%; 43 of 48). Senate Democrats scored an average of only 1%. Most Democrats scored 0% (94%; 48 of 51). They voted

---

[85] Ibid.

against Christian values on all issues.[86] House Republicans scored an average of 98%. Most Republicans scored 100% (94%; 229 of 243). Most Democrats scored 0% (88%; 171 of 194). They voted against Christian values on all issues.[87]

Knowing these facts raises the same questions raised by the "Vote Scorecard" developed by Focus Action and Family Research Council Action. How can any Christian vote for any Democrat knowing that Democrats are so united in voting against Christian values? How can any Christian do anything that would help put Democrats in power, knowing that they would govern totally contrary to simple, basic moral laws revealed by God through Scripture? Voting for most Democrats or doing anything that would put Democrats is totally contrary to what it means to be a Christian.

---

[86] National Right to Life Committee, "Federal NRLC Scorecard - 110th Congress, Combined Sessions," http://www.nrlc.org (accessed July 21, 2012).
[87] Ibid.

CHAPTER 3.0

LIVING AND VOTING CHRISTIAN VALUES

SECTION REVIEW. This section lays the foundation for the book. The first chapter discusses basic principles of living and voting Christian values. The second chapter defines what it means to be a Christian. The third chapter reviews the vital importance of scripture as the foundation for living the Christian life. The fourth chapter discusses how biblical law provides guidance for living and voting Christian values.

CHAPTERS:
3.1 Principles of Living Christian Values
3.2 Defining Christian
3.3 Scripture for Living Christian Values
3.4 Biblical Law for Living Christian Values

PRINCIPLES OF LIVING AND VOTING CHRISTIAN VALUES

LIVING CHRISTIAN VALUES. Being a Christian requires living and voting Christian values. Most Christian leaders teach that men are saved by faith not works. Few teach that "faith without works is dead" (James 2:20; 2:26). Christ said,

> Not every one that saith unto me, "Lord, Lord," shall enter into the kingdom of heaven; but he that doeth the will of my Father which is in heaven. Many will say to me in that day, "Lord, Lord, have we not prophesied in thy name? and in thy name have cast out devils? and in thy name done many wonderful works?" And then will I profess unto them, I never knew you: depart from me, ye that work iniquity (Matt. 7:21-23, KJV).

On Judgment Day Christ will reject many Americans who call themselves Christians because they did not" do the will of [the] Father," they did not live Christian values.

DEFINING CHRISTIAN. A Christian is not simply someone who believes in Christ. A Christian is a follower of Christ. A Christian is a repentant sinner who dies to self and lives for Christ, someone who can join the Apostle Paul in saying, "For to me to live is Christ, and to die is gain" (Phil. 1:20-22). In other words, a man who claims to be a Christian is not a Christian unless Christ is his reason for living. See chapter on definition of Christian for more detailed explanation.

LIVING BY FAITH. God has ordained that man must live by faith. "The fool hath said in his heart, 'There is no God'" (Ps. 14:1; 53:1, KJV). A college professor who claims that only weak people need belief in a God is a fool who deliberately ignores the self-evident truth that there is a God. There is infinitely more scientific evidence in support of God and creation than evolution. Romans teaches that blindness is a result of a decision to ignore clear evidence of God revealed through creation.

The just shall live by faith. For the wrath of God is revealed from heaven against all ungodliness and unrighteousness of men, who hold the truth in unrighteousness; because that which may be known of God is manifest in them; for God hath shewed it unto them. For the invisible things of him from the creation of the world are clearly seen, being understood by the things that are made, even his eternal power and Godhead; so that they are without excuse: because that, when they knew God, they glorified him not as God, neither were thankful; but became vain in their imaginations, and their foolish heart was darkened. Professing themselves to be wise, they became fools (Rom. 1:17-22).

FAITH AND REASON FOR LIVING. I describe a man's faith or religion as his reason for living. Every man has a faith or religion, which is his reason for living. How a person lives says more about their true faith, their real reason for living, than whether they claim to be a Christian or attend church. A man who claims to be a Christian and attends church every week but lives totally contrary to scripture is not a Christian.

POLITICS AS FAITH IN ACTION. Politics is faith in action. Voting Christian values is part of living Christian values. How a man votes says more about his real faith, his real reason for living, than whether or not he claims to be a Christian or attends church.

MISSION. The primary God-given mission of Christians is not to win souls for Christ or to make disciples of all nations or to love their fellow man as they love themselves. The primary God-given mission of every man, woman, and child is to "love the Lord our God with all your heart, mind, soul, and strength" (Luke Mt. 22:37-40). Loving God requires obedience to God's will and God's commandments. Christ said, "My food is to do the will of Him who sent me." All Christians should have the exact same attitude. Their first and foremost desire should be to do God's will at all times, to include when voting.

KING DAVID. One of the most amazing verses in Scripture contains the words of King David after he was confronted by the prophet Nathan. "Against Thee and only Thee have I sinned." After committing murder and adultery, why did King David say that he had only sinned against God? Answer: King David, the only man described in scripture as "a man after God's heart," understood that every thought, word, and action is first and foremost a thought, word, or action for or against God, not for or against his fellow man. Likewise every vote is first and foremost a vote for or against God.

FREEDOM. Most Americans have a totally different understanding of freedom than that given by God in scripture. Most believe that freedom is the right to do whatever is right in your own eyes, so long as doing so does not harm another person. That is totally contrary to Scripture. The words, "Every man did that which was right in his own eyes" (Judges 17:5-7; 21:24-25) describe a period of lawlessness in Israel (See Deut. 12:7-9; Prov. 12:15; 21:2). God commanded the Israelites to not do whatever was right in their own eyes, but to obey His commandments. King David said, "I will walk at liberty: for I seek thy precepts" (Ps. 119:45). In other words, true freedom is found through submission to God and obedience to His laws, not through doing whatever is right in your own eyes.

VOTING SCRIPTURE. Christ said, "Ye do err, not knowing the Scriptures, nor the power of God" (Matt. 22:28-30, KJV). Christ was talking about the Old Testament. The New Testament was written after Christ's death and resurrection. " Living and voting Christian values requires living and voting in accordance with Scripture, which includes the Old Testament. See Chapter on Scripture for more detailed discussion.

VOTING BIBLICAL LAW. Living and voting Christian values requires living and voting in accordance with biblical law. Christ said,"Think not that I am come to destroy the law, or the prophets: I am not come to destroy, but to fulfill...." (Matt. 5:17-18, KJV). King David said, "Thy word is a lamp unto my feet, and a light unto my path" (Psalms 119:105) and "I will walk at liberty: for I seek thy precepts" (Psalms 119:45, KJV). See chapter on Biblical Law for scripture and detailed explanation.

ARMOR OF GOD. Christians are called by God to be salt and light to the world in our schools, workplace, government, and all other areas of life. Christians are called to put on the full armor of God and to do battle for the Lord in all areas of life. Our nation is greatly in need of more Christians willing to be salt and light and do battle in politics, law, and government.

DEFINING CHRISTIAN

REASON FOR CHAPTER. Most Americans cannot give an accurate definition of "Christian." Non-Christians have a totally flawed understanding what it means to be a Christian and what freedom of religion requires. Many Christians think that simply believing in Christ as Savior makes one a Christian. This is totally contrary to the teachings of Christ.

FIRST ELEMENT. There are several essential elements of being a Christian. First, a Christian is someone who, like all Jews and Muslims, believes in God. He understands that:

1. There is one true God, who always was, is, and ever shall be.
2. He never changes. He is the same yesterday, today, and tomorrow.
3. He created all things seen and unseen, and all laws that govern all things seen and unseen.
4. He creates each man in His own image, knitting him together in his mother's womb.

A Christian understands that God's moral laws are rooted in His unchanging character. They do not change or evolve. They are the same today as they were when our universe was created. These include laws that govern men and governments. The United States was founded upon these self-evident, common sense truths, revealed by God through creation and embodied in the Declaration of Independence and U.S. Constitution.

SECOND ELEMENT. Second, a Christian is someone who, unlike Jews or Muslims, believes in a triune God, one God in three persons: Father, Son, and Holy Spirit. This is not common sense. It is not revealed through creation. It is revealed through Scripture, and it takes a special gift of faith from God to believe.

Many Christians publicly profess their faith in the God the Father, Son, and Holy Spirit through the Apostles' Creed, which briefly summarizes key tenants of the Christian faith.

1. I believe in God, the Father almighty, creator of heaven and earth.
2. I believe in Jesus Christ, His only Son, our Lord.
3. He was conceived by the power of the Holy Spirit and born of the Virgin Mary.
4. He suffered under Pontius Pilate, was crucified, died, and was buried.
5. He descended to the dead. On the third day he rose again.
6. He ascended into heaven and is seated at the right hand of the Father.
7. He will come again to judge the living and the dead.
8. I believe in the Holy Spirit,
9. the holy Catholic Church, the communion of saints,
10. the forgiveness of sins,
11. the resurrection of the body,
12. and life everlasting. Amen.[88]

---

[88] The *Catechism of the Catholic Church* gives this English translation of the Apostles' Creed. The Catechism maintains the traditional division into twelve articles. See http://en.wikipedia.org/wiki/Apostles%27_Creed.

A Christian believes that Christ is the Son of God and the Messiah and Savior whose coming was prophesied to the people of Israel. He believes that Christ is fully God and fully man and that if He was not both He could not be the perfect, blameless "Lamb of God" who made payment in full for the sins of man through His death on the cross. However, belief in all the foregoing does not make one a Christian. Satan and his demons believe in God; it does not make them Christians.

THIRD ELEMENT. Third, a Christian is a repentant sinner. "I love being Catholic, because I can do whatever I want and just go to confession," said a young lady. She is the perfect example of someone who is not a Christian because he or she is not repentant. No priest has the power to forgive the sins of anyone who is not repentant. Repentance means more than true regret for sin; it means turning from sin to obedience to God. King David provides the best example of true repentance:

> Have mercy upon me, O God, according to thy
> lovingkindness: according unto the
> multitude of thy tender mercies blot out
> my transgressions.
> Wash me thoroughly from mine iniquity, and
> cleanse me from my sin.
> For I acknowledge my transgressions: and my
> sin is ever before me.
> Against thee, thee only, have I sinned, and done
> this evil in thy sight: that thou mightest
> be justified when thou speakest, and be
> clear when thou judgest.
> Behold, I was shapen in iniquity; and in sin did
> my mother conceive me.

Behold, thou desirest truth in the inward parts:
and in the hidden part thou shalt make
me to know wisdom.

Purge me with hyssop, and I shall be clean:
wash me, and I shall be whiter than
snow.

Make me to hear joy and gladness; that the
bones which thou hast broken may
rejoice.

Hide thy face from my sins, and blot out all
mine iniquities.

Create in me a clean heart, O God; and renew a
right spirit within me.

Cast me not away from thy presence; and take
not thy Holy Spirit from me.

Restore unto me the joy of thy salvation; and
uphold me with thy free spirit.

Then will I teach transgressors thy ways; and
sinners shall be converted unto thee.

Deliver me from bloodguiltiness, O God, thou
God of my salvation: and my tongue
shall sing aloud of thy righteousness.

O Lord, open thou my lips; and my mouth shall
shew forth thy praise.

For thou desirest not sacrifice; else would I give
it: thou delightest not in burnt offering.

The sacrifices of God are a broken spirit: a
broken and a contrite heart, O God, thou
wilt not despise.

Do good in thy good pleasure unto Zion: build
thou the walls of Jerusalem.

Then shalt thou be pleased with the sacrifices of
righteousness, with burnt offering and
whole burnt offering: then shall they

offer bullocks upon thine altar. Psalm 51:1-19 (KJV).

Note that true repentance requires: (1) full acknowledgment of sin against God; (2) true regret for sin against God; (3) humble request for God's forgiveness; (4) cleansing and full restoration of relationship with God; (5) empowerment by God to do His will; (6) humble obedience to God's will.

FOURTH ELEMENT. Fourth, a Christian is someone who accepts Christ as Savior. He understands that God is holy, and that no man can meet God's standard of perfection. He understands that "all have sinned, and come short of the glory of God" (Rom 3:22-24). He understands that only Christ, the perfect Lamb of God, fully God and fully man, could make payment for man's sins. He understands that Christ died on the cross as payment in full for his sins, and that he can only be cleansed by faith in what Christ has done for him. "For God so loved the world, that he gave his only begotten Son, that whosoever believeth in him should not perish, but have everlasting life" (John 3:16, KJV). He knows that "a man is not justified by the works of the law, but by the faith of Jesus Christ" (Gal 2:16, KJV). Therefore he accepts Christ as his Savior, as the Lamb of God who made payment in full for his sins through death on the cross.

FIFTH ELEMENT. Fifth, a Christian is someone who accepts Christ as the Lord of his life. Christ said, "If any man will come after me, let him deny himself, and take up his cross, and follow me" (Mat. 16:23-25, KJV). He said, "And he that taketh not his cross, and followeth after me, is not worthy of me" (Matt. 10:38, KJV. See also Mark 8:34-35, Luke 9:22-24, KJV). Christ said, "My food is to do the will of Him who sent

Me, and to finish His work" (John 4:34, NKJV). If a man believes in Christ and accepts Him as the Lord of his life, then he will take up his cross, dying to self, and follow Him.

Christ made it clear that one cannot be a Christian, a follower of Christ, and live contrary to God's commandments.

> Not every one that saith unto me, "Lord, Lord," shall enter into the kingdom of heaven; but he that doeth the will of my Father which is in heaven. Many will say to me in that day, "Lord, Lord, have we not prophesied in thy name? and in thy name have cast out devils? and in thy name done many wonderful works?" And then will I profess unto them, I never knew you: depart from me, ye that work iniquity (Matt. 7:21-23, KJV).

In other words, believing in Christ as Lord and Savior and doing great miracles in His name does not make one a Christian. A Christian is a follower of Christ who does "the will of my Father." Doing God's will means living and in obedience to His commandments. This does not mean that anyone is saved by works. Man is saved by faith not works, but "faith without works is dead" (James 2:20, KJV; see also James 2:17, 25-26). A man who chooses to live contrary to God's commandments is not a Christian because he is not repentant and he has not accepted Christ as Lord and Savior.

SIXTH ELEMENT. Sixth, a Christian is empowered and guided by the Spirit of God (the Holy Spirit). Jesus made it clear that being saved required being "born again" and that this spiritual rebirth required not just baptism with water, but being "born of...the Spirit." He said, "Except a man be born of water and of the Spirit, he cannot enter into the kingdom of God. That which is born of the flesh is flesh; and that which is born of the Spirit is spirit. Marvel not that I said unto thee, 'Ye must be born again'" (John 3:5-7, KJV).

When Christ gave the Great Commission to his disciples, he said, "All power is given unto me in heaven and in earth. Go ye therefore, and teach all nations, baptizing them in the name of the Father, and of the Son, and of the Holy Ghost: Teaching them to observe all things whatsoever I have commanded you..." (Matt. 28:18-20, KJV). Baptism in the name of the Spirit (Holy Ghost) had special meaning. Jesus said, "For John truly baptized with water; but ye shall be baptized with the Holy Ghost.... But ye shall receive power, after that the Holy Ghost is come upon you: and ye shall be witnesses unto me...unto the uttermost part of the earth" (Act 1:5-8, KJV). In other words, part of being saved involved being "baptized with the Holy Ghost", which resulted in being empowered by the Holy Spirit.

John states that believers in Christ would receive the "Spirit" ("Holy Ghost"). First he quotes Christ; then he explains the meaning of Christ's words (in parentheses): " He that believeth on me, as the Scripture hath said, out of his belly shall flow rivers of living water. (But this spake he of the Spirit, which they that believe on him should receive: for the Holy Ghost was not yet given; because that Jesus was not yet glorified)" (John 7:38-39, KJV). Acts 5:32 refers to the Holy Spirit as "the Holy Ghost, whom God hath given to them that obey him" (Acts 5:32, KJV). In other words, being saved requires obedience to God's commandments, and God gives His Holy Spirit to those who are saved and therefore obedient to His will.

The Apostle Paul explains in great detail the role of the Spirit of God in empowering and guiding the believer to do the will of God.

> For they that are after the flesh do mind the things of the flesh; but they that are after the Spirit the things of the Spirit. For to be carnally minded is death; but to be spiritually minded is life and peace. Because the carnal mind is enmity against God: for it is not subject to the law of God, neither indeed can be. So then they that are in the flesh cannot please God. But ye are not in the flesh, but in the Spirit, if so be that the Spirit of God dwell in you. Now if any man have not the Spirit of Christ, he is none of his. And if Christ be in you, the body is dead because of sin; but the Spirit is life because of righteousness. But if the Spirit of him that raised up Jesus from the dead dwell in you, he that raised up Christ from the dead shall also quicken your mortal bodies by his Spirit that dwelleth in you. Therefore, brethren, we are debtors, not to the flesh, to live after the flesh. For if ye live after the flesh, ye shall die: but if ye through the Spirit do mortify the deeds of the body, ye shall live. For as many as are led by the Spirit of God, they are the sons of God (Rom 1:5-14, KJV).

SEVENTH ELEMENT. Seventh, a Christian is a person whose reason for living is Christ. Paul said, "For to me to live is Christ, and to die is gain"(Phil. 1:20-22). Christ said, "My meat is to do the will of him that sent me, and to finish his work" (John 4:34, KJV). Christ and Paul provide perfect examples of the total devotion and commitment required by someone whose reason for living is loving and serving God.

Christ also said, "He that loveth father or mother more than me is not worthy of me: and he that loveth son or daughter more than me is not worthy of me" (Matt. 10:36-38, KJV). If loving and serving God is not a man's top priority and primary objective, his reason for living, then he is in violation of the greatest commandment: "Thou shalt love the Lord thy God with all thy heart, and with all thy soul, and with all thy might" (Deut. 6:5, KJV. See also Matt. 22:37-38; Luke 10:27). He is also in violation of the first of the ten commandments: "Thou shalt have none other gods before me" (Deut. 5:7, KJV).

The author defines a man's faith or religion as his reason for living. Everyone has a faith or religion, a reason for living. A man's true faith or religion is the true reason he lives and votes that way that he does. A man who claims to be a Christian and attends church weekly but lives and votes contrary to Christian values is not a Christian.

CONCLUSION. Contrary to popular opinion, a Christian is not simply someone who believes in God or someone who accepts Christ as Savior. A Christian is someone who: (1) believes one true God, the Creator of all things seen and unseen (2) believes in a triune God, one God in three persons: Father, Son, and Holy Spirit; (3) is a repentant sinner; (4) is saved by faith in Christ as his Savior; (5) accepts Christ as the Lord of his life; (6) is empowered and guided by the Holy Spirit; and (7) is a person whose reason for living is Christ.

CHAPTER 3.3

SCRIPTURE AND LIVING CHRISTIAN VALUES

LEADING QUESTION. "What is the one thing that I want you to believe more than anything else?" I asked my three daughters. The answer, I explained, was not God or Christ, but Scripture. Why?

FIRST REASON. God reveals Himself to man through Scripture. Without Scripture every man must imagine God in his own mind, and everyone gets it wrong in so many ways. Why is knowledge of God so important? Understanding of God, the Creator of all things seen and unseen, is the foundation for understanding of the meaning and purpose of all things seen and unseen. Americans today, including Christians, are at an all time low for understanding of God and the meaning and purpose of their own lives. On Judgment Day most Americans will face the wrath of a holy, righteous God, in part because they never understood God or what He requires of man.

SECOND REASON. Second, God uses Scripture to reveal Christ to man. It gives prophecy regarding Christ and tells the story of His birth, life, death, and resurrection. God uses Scripture not only to give facts about Christ, but also, by telling the story of the life of Christ, to give the perfect example of what it means to be a Christian, a follower of Christ. Christ also provides an example of someone who understood the importance of Old Testament Scripture and studied it so diligently that as a young boy He knew more than the priests in the temple. He quoted it throughout His ministry.

THIRD REASON. Third, Scripture reveals what is required to become a Christian, a follower of Christ, through the words of Christ, Matthew, Mark, Luke, John, Paul, Peter, and other authors of Scripture. The Apostle Paul refers to "the holy Scriptures, which are able to make thee wise unto salvation through faith which is in Christ Jesus" (2 Tim. 3:15, KJV). The chapter entitled "Defining Christian" discusses the elements of being a Christian.

FOURTH REASON. Fourth, God uses Scripture to give the facts regarding the history ("His story") of the world and of His workings with His people and others from creation to Christ's birth, life, death, and resurrection and to the time of Christ's return to earth in glory.

FIFTH REASON. Fifth, God gives Christians the guidance they need to live the Christian life through laws and principles revealed in Scripture, through the words of Moses, King David, King Solomon, the prophets, Christ, Paul, and other authors of Scripture. Paul said, "All Scripture is given by inspiration of God, and is profitable for doctrine, for reproof, for correction, for instruction in righteousness" (2 Tim. 3:16, KJV).

Without Scripture, every man does whatever is right in his own eyes, and even the most intelligent get it so very wrong. The words, "Every man did that which was right in his own eyes" (Judges 17:5-7; 21:24-25) describe a period of lawlessness in Israel (See Deut. 12:7-9; Prov. 12:15; 21:2). Proverbs states, "The way of a fool is right in his own eyes: but he that hearken[s] unto counsel is wise" (Prov.12:14-16) and "there is a way which seem[s] right unto a man, but the end thereof are the ways of death (Prov. 14:12; 16:25). God spoke through Isaiah saying, "For my thoughts are not your thoughts, neither are your ways my ways, saith the LORD. For as the heavens are higher than the earth, so are my ways higher than your ways, and my thoughts than your thoughts (Isa. 55:8-10). Jesus said, "Ye do err, not knowing the Scriptures, nor the power of God" (Matt. 22:29, KJV). Often what seems right to even the most intelligent of men is totally contrary to God's ways, because God's ways are higher than man's ways. The perfect example is President Obama, as will be shown, a very intelligent man with the best of intentions who fights for policies totally contrary to God's laws.

CONCLUSION. Belief in Scripture is more important than belief in God or Christ because Scripture defines God, Christ, and what it means to be a Christian. Every law student, lawyer, and judge studies two aspects of every case: the facts and the law. God uses Scripture to give man the facts and the law needed for living the Christian life. Without Scripture even Christians have totally wrong and conflicting opinions of God, Christ, what it means to be a Christian, and what it means to live and vote Christian values. Scripture is a very special gift of God to man, given because God knew man desperately needed written guidance for godly living. Men seek freedom through rebellion against God's law, through doing whatever is right in their own eyes. But true freedom and blessings only come through obedience to God's laws. That is why King David said, "Thy word is a lamp unto my feet, and a light unto my path" (Psalms 119:105) and "I will walk at liberty: for I seek thy precepts" (Psalms 119:45, KJV).

BIBLICAL LAW AND LIVING CHRISTIAN VALUES

REASON FOR CHAPTER. Why does a chapter entitled "Biblical Law" immediately follow a chapter entitled "Defining Christian?" A Christian is by definition a follower of Christ who wants to love and serve God by doing "the will of the Father" by being obedient to God's laws revealed through Scripture. In other words, Christians need Scripture to live the Christian life. That is why Christ said, "Ye do err, not knowing the Scriptures, nor the power of God" (Matt. 22:28-30, KJV).

Many Christians and Christian leaders are surprisingly ignorant regarding basic principles of biblical law. There is very little emphasis on biblical law in seminaries, and many men in the ministry have little interest in law, politics, business, jobs, the economy, etc. They live in a different world and fail to provide the guidance that God offers through Scripture regarding these areas. Many concentrate on the love of God and neglect His holiness and righteousness. They fail to properly challenge Americans who live in a fantasy world where a loving God would never punish "good" people. Christians and Christian leaders fail to realize that study of biblical law provides amazing, fascinating insight into the heart and mind of God in many areas of life where they desperately need His guidance.

OLD TESTAMENT LAW. Some Christians claim that Jesus showed that Old Testament law should no longer be applied when He forgave the woman caught in adultery. The

Pharisees tried to trap Jesus, knowing that the law called for stoning. Jesus evaded their trap by writing in the sand until all of the woman's accusers left. Then He said "Neither do I condemn thee: go, and sin no more"(John 8:10-12, KJV). However, Jesus was not a government official with authority or responsibility to impose punishment. Even a judge would not have authority to render judgment and impose the death penalty without a trial. When Christ returns, he will judge everyone.

Many Christians believe that Old Testament law is part of the Old Covenant that God had with the nation of Israel, and that it was replaced by the New Testament or New Covenant, which does not require obedience to Old Testament law. Some clergy might point to verses that seem to imply that the law was just a tutor to point sinners to Christ. "So that the law is become our tutor to bring us unto Christ, that we might be justified by faith. But now faith that is come, we are no longer under a tutor" (Gal. 3:24-25, ASV). "No longer under a tutor" means no longer under the law. However, assuming that one can therefore ignore the law would be totally contrary to the teachings of Christ and Scripture. God cares just as much about obedience to His laws today as when he killed thousands of His own people for what many today would consider minor disobedience.

Many Christians and religious leaders do not understand how Old Testament law applies to modern times. Christ said,"Think not that I am come to destroy the law, or the prophets: I am not come to destroy, but to fulfill. For verily I say unto you, till heaven and earth pass, one jot or one tittle shall in no wise pass from the law, till all be fulfilled" (Matt. 5:17-18, KJV). The law and the prophets are the books of law and the prophets in the Old Testament. The "jot" and "tittle" are the smallest parts of the Hebrew alphabet, similar to the dot on an "i" and apostrophe in the English language. Christ made it clear that He did not come to destroy Old Testament law, but to fulfill it, and that not even the smallest part of the law would "pass" until it was "fulfilled." As one of my professors in graduate school said, God the Father was not converted by Christ the Son. Christ's coming did not do away with Old Testament law. It fulfilled Old Testament laws related to payment for sin, because He was the Lamb of God who gave His life as payment for sin, but all other laws remained in full effect.

LOVING GOD. As noted in the Introduction, the most important biblical law is the Greatest Commandment, first stated by Moses: "Thou shalt love the Lord thy God with all thy heart, and with all thy soul, and with all thy might" (Deut. 6:5, KJV). Christ said: "Thou shalt love the Lord thy God with all thy heart, and with all thy soul, and with all thy mind. This is the first and great commandment" (Matt. 22:37-38, KJV; see Luke 10:27).

Many Old and New Testament passages state that loving God requires obedience to his commandments. "For this is the love of God, that we keep his commandments: and his commandments are not grievous" (1 John 5:3, KJV). "If ye love me, keep my commandments" (John 14:15, KJV). "He that hath my commandments, and keepeth them, he it is that loveth me: and he that loveth me shall be loved of my Father, and I will love him, and will manifest myself to him" John 14:21 (KJV). "Therefore thou shalt love the LORD thy God, and keep his charge, and his statutes, and his judgments, and his commandments, always" (Deut. 11:1, KJV). "In that I command thee this day to love the LORD thy God, to walk in his ways, and to keep his commandments and his statutes and his judgments, that thou mayest live and multiply: and the LORD thy God shall bless thee in the land whither thou goest to possess it" (Deut. 30:16, KJV). "But take diligent heed to do the commandment and the law, which Moses the servant of the LORD charged you, to love the LORD your God, and to walk in all his ways, and to keep his commandments, and to cleave unto him, and to serve him with all your heart and with all your soul" (Joshua 22:5, KJV).

Four of the most important commandments that deal with loving God are the first four of the Ten Commandments:

> I am the LORD thy God, which brought thee out of the land of Egypt, from the house of bondage.
> [First Commandment] Thou shalt have none other gods before me.
> [Second Commandment] Thou shalt not make thee any graven ...for I the LORD thy God am a jealous God, visiting the iniquity of the fathers upon the children unto the third and fourth generation of them that hate me, And shewing mercy unto thousands of them that love me and keep my commandments.
> [Third Commandment] Thou shalt not take the name of the LORD thy God in vain: for the LORD will not hold him guiltless that taketh his name in vain.
> [Fourth Commandment] Keep the sabbath day to sanctify it... (Deut. 5:6-15, KJV).

Note that God brings terrible judgment upon those who hate Him, "visiting the iniquity of the fathers upon the children unto the third and fourth generation of them that hate me," but shows great mercy toward those who love him, "shewing mercy unto thousands of them that love me and keep my commandments" (Deut. 5:9-10, KJV). Many passages state that God shows love and mercy to those who love Him and keep his commandments (Ex. 20:6; Deut. 5:10; 7:9; 11:1-2, 13-14, 22-23; 19:9; Josh. 22:5-6; Neh. 1:5; Dan. 9:4; John 14:21; 15:10). Deuteronomy 7:9 (KJV) states: "Know therefore that the LORD thy God, he is God, the faithful God, which keepeth covenant and mercy with them that love him and keep his commandments to a thousand generations."

LOVING MAN. After Christ quoted the greatest commandment, He added the second greatest commandment.

> Jesus said unto him, Thou shalt love the Lord
> thy God with all thy heart, and with all thy soul,
> and with all thy mind. This is the first and great
> commandment. And the second is like unto it,
> Thou shalt love thy neighbour as thyself. On
> these two commandments hang all the law and
> the prophets (Matthew 22:37-40, KJV).

Note Christ's final words: "On these two commandments hang all the law and the prophets" (Matt. 22:40, KJV). The law and the prophets are the books of law and books of the prophets of the Old Testament, which contain Old Testament law. Thus Christ affirmed that all Old Testament law, which remains in effect, "hangs" on these two commandments.

The primary means of loving one's neighbor is obedience to the many commandments given through Scripture related to treatment of others. "And this is love, that we walk after his commandments. This is the commandment, That, as ye have heard from the beginning, ye should walk in it" (2 John 1:6, KJV). "By this we know that we love the children of God, when we love God, and keep his commandments" (1

John 5:2, KJV). Examples commandment related to loving one's neighbor include the final six of the ten commandments.

> [Fifth Commandment] Honour thy father and thy mother, as the LORD thy God hath commanded thee; that thy days may be prolonged, and that it may go well with thee, in the land which the LORD thy God giveth thee.
> [Sixth Commandment] Thou shalt not kill.
> [Seventh Commandment] Neither shalt thou commit adultery.
> [Eighth Commandment] Neither shalt thou steal.
> [Ninth Commandment] Neither shalt thou bear false witness against thy neighbour.
> [Tenth Commandment] Neither shalt thou desire thy neigh[bor]s wife, neither shalt thou covet thy neigh[bor]'s house, his field, or his manservant, or his maidservant, his ox, or his ass, or any thing that is thy neigh[bor]'s. (Deut. 5:16-21, KJV).

HIGHER STANDARD. After declaring that He came not to destroy Old Testament law, but to fulfill it, Christ introduced a higher standard. First He clarified the importance of obedience to even the "least commandments." Then he reviewed many points of Old Testament law, and showed that he required even higher standards.

> Whosoever...shall break one of these least commandments, and shall teach men so, he shall be called the least in the kingdom of heaven: but whosoever shall do and teach them, the same shall be called great in the kingdom of heaven.... Ye have heard that it was said...Thou shalt not kill; and whosoever shall kill shall be in danger of the judgment:

69

"But I say unto you, That whosoever is angry with his brother without a cause shall be in danger of the judgment.... Ye have heard that it was said... Thou shalt not commit adultery: But I say unto you, That whosoever looketh on a woman to lust after her hath committed adultery with her already in his heart.... It hath been said, Whosoever shall put away his wife, let him give her a writing of divorcement: But I say unto you, That whosoever shall put away his wife, saving for the cause of fornication, causeth her to commit adultery: and whosoever shall marry her that is divorced commit[s] adultery. Again, ye have heard that it hath been said... Thou shalt not forswear thyself, but shalt perform unto the Lord thine oaths: But I say unto you, Swear not at all.... But let your communication be, Yea, yea; Nay, nay: for whatsoever is more than these cometh of evil. Ye have heard that it hath been said, An eye for an eye, and a tooth for a tooth: But I say unto you, That ye resist not evil: but whosoever shall smite thee on thy right cheek, turn to him the other also.... Ye have heard that it hath been said, Thou shalt love thy neighbour, and hate thine enemy. But I say unto you, Love your enemies, bless them that curse you, do good to them that hate you, and pray for them which despitefully use you, and persecute you; That ye may be the children of your Father which is in heaven .... Be ye therefore perfect, even as your Father which is in heaven is perfect (Matt. 5:17-49, KJV).

Christ established higher standards for murder, adultery, divorce, justice and mercy, and loving one's enemies. Then He gave the clincher, the bottom line, the principle that should govern the life of every Christian: "Be ye therefore perfect, even as your Father which is in heaven is perfect"

(Matthew 5:49, KJV). In other words, Christians are called to be perfect not only through complete obedience to the letter of Old Testament law (every jot and title), but also through complete obedience to the much higher standard of the true spirit and intent of the law, as taught and lived by Christ. No Christian can be perfect like God the Father, but every Christian is commanded by Christ to strive for perfection. This means getting up after falling, repenting of wrongdoing, and continuing to run the race which Christians are called to run, striving for perfection.

CONCLUSION. So what does all this have to do with politics and elections? God provides much needed guidance to man through biblical law revealed through Scripture. Without biblical law, man cannot properly discern right from wrong. Being a Christian requires more than just believing in Christ as Lord and Savior. It requires taking up one's cross and following Christ, dying to self and living for Christ, and being obedient to God's commandments. These commandments include all Old Testament and New Testament laws not fulfilled by the coming of Christ. Christ only fulfilled laws regarding sacrifice, because He was the Lamb of God, the final, perfect sacrifice. Christ made it perfectly clear that He did not come to abolish the law, but to fulfill it, and gave an even higher standard for obedience to biblical law revealed through the Old Testament, the only Scripture that existed at the time of Christ. Being a Christian requires voting for candidates that support God's laws revealed through Scripture.

VOTING FOR THE SUPREME COURT

INTRODUCTION. The most important consideration in voting for president in 2016 is the Supreme Court. One of the greatest and most important powers of the President is the ability to appoint Supreme Court justices who serve for life. A president may serve only four years. His decisions may be reversed by the next president. A Supreme Court Justice may serve 20 to 30 years, and his rulings dramatically affect the lives of Americans for countless years after the President is no longer in office.

Republicans, in total contrast to Democrats, support the appointment of federal judges and Supreme Court Justices who will uphold the Constitution of the United States and not try to legislate from the bench.[89] Legislation, making law, is the duty of elected members of the legislature, which at the federal level is Congress (Senate and House of Representatives).

No Democrat will appoint a Supreme Court justice who will uphold the Constitution, because doing so would be totally contrary to deeply-rooted values of all Democrats. The primary purpose of the Constitution is to define the limits of power of the federal government. Democrats will only support justices who completely ignore those limits of power, granting totally unconstitutional education and healthcare benefits. The Supreme Court justices they appoint will use the interstate commerce clause, taxation clause (Obamacare), and other parts of the Constitution to justify actions by Congress that are

---

[89] "2012 Values Voter Presidential Voter Guide," Family Research Council Action, http://www.frcaction.org (accessed August 3, 2012).

totally contrary to the Constitution. See chapters on Constitution, Democratic Platform, and Biblical Role of Government for more detailed discussion.

APPOINTMENTS OF PRESIDENT OBAMA. Few Presidents in the history of the United States have violated the Constitution more than President Obama. No President has appointed two Supreme Court justices who rule so totally contrary to Scripture and the Constitution. If another Democrat chooses Justice Scalia's replacement, the United States will suffer the negative results for generations.

During his first two years in office, President Obama replaced 2 of the 9 Supreme Court Justices, as many as President George W. Bush replaced in 8 years. Obama's advisors were "preparing for the possibility of a third vacancy, which could make his imprint even more indelible."[90]

In 2009 President Obama appointed Sonia Sotomayor to the U.S. Supreme Court. Sotomayor helped direct litigation of a private organization that filed many pro-abortion lawsuits, to include challenges to parental notification requirements.[91] Tony Perkins, President of Family Research Council, said:

> President Obama has chosen a nominee with a compelling personal story over a judicial pick with a solid judicial philosophy…. Judge Sotomayor's failure to premise her decisions on the text of the Constitution has resulted in an extremely high rate of reversal before the high court to which she has been nominated…. Judge Sotomayor appears to

---

[90] "Where Do the Candidates Stand on Life: Mitt Romney, Barack Obama."
[91] "The Presidential Record on Life: President Barack Obama 2009-present," National Right to Life, http://www.nrlc.org.

subscribe to a very liberal judicial philosophy that considers it appropriate for judges to impose their personal views from the bench. President Obama promised us a jurist committed to the "rule of law," but, instead, he appears to have nominated a legislator to the Supreme Court.... In a 2005 panel discussion at the Duke University Law School...the judge stated that the U.S. Court of Appeals is "where policy is made".... Our constitution states otherwise and public surveys indicate that the American public understands this constitutional principle and wants judges who interpret the law and do not act as life-tenured judicially empowered social workers. [92]

In other words, Judge Sotomayor is an extremely liberal judge who believes in making policy and legislating from the bench, totally contrary to her duty to interpret and apply the law to the facts of each case. Legislation, making law, is the duty of elected members of the legislature, which at the federal level is Congress i.e. the Senate and House of Representatives.

On May 11, 2010, the Washington Post announced President Obama's appointment of Elena Kagan, a woman who never served as a judge at any level and only short time as Solicitor General, to the Supreme Court. As former Dean of Harvard Law School, Kagan barred Armed Forces recruiters from the Law School's Office of Career Services in protest of the "Don't ask, don't tell" policy regarding homosexuals serving in the Armed Forces.[93] As a key political aide to

---

[92] "Sotomayor: A Policy Maker or a Jurist?", Family Research Council Action, May 26, 2009, http://www.frcaction.org.
[93] Jonathan Blakely, "One Top GOP Line of Attack: Kagan's Opposition to Military Recruitment at Harvard Law School's Office of Career Services,"

President Clinton, Kagan helped direct a political strategy that would nullify a ban on partial-birth abortions during the Clinton Administration.[94]

Tony Perkins, President of Family Research Council, said:

> Throughout her career, Ms. Kagan has supported the promotion of abortion, even if it includes funding with American tax dollars. She publicly disagreed with the decision in Rust v. Sullivan that gave the government the right to deny taxpayer funds to groups that perform or promote abortions. A large majority of Americans disagree with her on that point, as did the Supreme Court.... Ms. Kagan's memo to President Bill Clinton in 1997...advised the President to support a "compromise" allowing for "health exceptions" to the ban on the gruesome and cruel procedure of partial birth abortion... a blatant attempt to create a giant loophole rendering the bill meaningless.[95]

In other words, Elena Kagan is a woman who never served as a judge and is a very strong supporter of partial birth abortion, taxpayer funding of abortion, and the homosexual lifestyle. She is absolutely, without any question whatsoever,

---

ABC News, http://abcnews.go.com/blogs/politics/2010/05/one-top-gop-line-of-attack-kagans-opposition-to-military-recruitment-at-harvard-law-schools-office-of-career-services/.

[94] "The Presidential Record on Life: President Barack Obama 2009-present," National Right to Life, http://www.nrlc.org.

[95] "FRC Action: Elena Kagan's Pro-Abortion Record is Far Outside the Mainstream", Family Research Council Action, May 19, 2010, http://www.frcaction.org.

the Supreme Court Justice who is least qualified to be on the U.S. Supreme Court.

A Washington Post article discussing the significance of the Kagan appointment stated:

> With his second Supreme Court nomination in as many years, <u>President Obama</u> has laid down clear markers <u>of his vision for the court, one that could prove to be among his most enduring legacies.</u> Together with Justice Sonia Sotomayor, <u>Elena Kagan</u>'s confirmation would represent a shift toward a younger, changing court, one that values experiences outside the courtroom and emphasizes personal interactions as much as deep knowledge of the law. Kagan, 50, the solicitor general named to replace outgoing liberal Justice John Paul Stevens, would…almost certainly provide a <u>lasting, liberal presence,</u> and administration officials hope she would, in the words of one, "<u>start to move the court into a different posture and profile.</u>"[96]

Advisers said that President Obama believed that "although Kagan has never been a judge, she would be able to play an "outsize role" on the bench by swaying her colleagues when opinion is divided."[97] Richard Garnett, law professor and associate dean of the University of Notre Dame Law School and former law clerk for Chief Justice William H.

---

[96] Anne E. Kornblut and Robert Barnes, "Kagan Would Emphasize Supreme Court Moving in New Direction," <u>The Washington Post</u>, May 11, 2010, http://www.washingtonpost.com/wp-dyn/content/article/2010/05/10/AR2010051001116.html.

[97] Anne E. Kornblut and Robert Barnes.

Rehnquist, said Obama was "poised to make a lasting impact on the court."

> The notion that he is just replacing one member of the so-called liberal wing with another, I think, is superficial…President Obama has a chance to <u>entrench his view of the Constitution for many years to come.</u>[98]

Why would President Obama appoint someone who never served as a judge on any court at any level to the highest court in the nation? Simply put, his objective was not to pick someone who would simply do the job of a judge, to interpret and apply the law to the facts of each case. His goal was to choose someone who could influence others to legislate from the bench and implement his policies.

<u>CONCLUSION</u>. President Obama appointed two extremely liberal justices who will continue to greatly influence the direction of our nation for many years after he is no longer in office. What are the consequences of appointment of liberal justices? Why should Americans care? First, liberal Supreme Court justices approve totally unconstitutional decisions of the President and Congress. These decisions increase taxes and reduce the freedom of religion and freedom of speech of Christians. Americans are forced to pay greater taxes to pay the education and healthcare bills of other Americans. Christians are forced to pay for abortions, abortive drugs, sterilization, contraceptives, and support homosexual couples by paying for their healthcare. Also, when Democrats have a majority in the Senate, they chair the Senate Judiciary Committee and block the nomination of pro-life, conservative Christians as federal judges and Supreme Court justices.

---

[98] Anne E. Kornblut and Robert Barnes.

CHAPTER 5.0

VOTING SCRIPTURE

SECTION REVIEW. This section discusses scripture on several key issues. Chapter 6.1 shows that God's ideal is not a government which cares for its people, or a government which discriminates based upon wealth or any other factor. Chapter 6.2 shows that God's ideal is the same tithe rate or "tax rate" for right and poor, and no discrimination based upon economic class. Chapter 6.3 shows that abortion is murder in the eyes of God. Chapter 6.4 shows that homosexuality and same-sex marriage are extreme perversions of God's design for man, woman, and marriage.

CHAPTERS:
5.1 Biblical Role of Government
5.2 Scripture on Taxes
5.3 Scripture on Abortion
5.4 Scripture on Homosexuality and
Same-Sex Marriage

CHAPTER 5.1

BIBLICAL ROLE OF GOVERNMENT

INTRODUCTION. "I believe that I am my brother's keeper." During the 2008 election, Senator Obama often used these words to explain what he believed to be the proper role of government, caring for its people. No other subject divides Christians between Republicans and Democrats more than the proper role of government. Most Democrats want a government that does more to take care of its people, especially the poor and the middle class. Most Republicans want a smaller federal government, which does less to care for its people. So who is right and who is wrong?

SCRIPTURE ON GOVERNMENT. What does God prefer, a government that does more to care for its people, or a government that does less? Does Scripture give any hint about God's ideal for government? First, consider 1 Samuel 8:4-22.

SCRIPTURE: 1 Samuel 8:4-22 (KJV):

Then all the elders of Israel gathered themselves together, and came to Samuel unto Ramah, and said unto him, "Behold, thou art old, and thy sons walk not in thy ways: now make us a king to judge us like all the nations." But the thing displeased Samuel, when they said, "Give us a king to judge us." And Samuel prayed unto the LORD. And the LORD said unto Samuel, "Hearken unto the voice of the people in all that they say unto thee: for they have not rejected thee, but they have rejected me, that I should not reign over them. According to all the works which they have done since the day that I brought them up out of Egypt even unto this day, wherewith they have forsaken me, and served other gods, so do they also unto thee. Now therefore hearken unto their voice: howbeit yet protest solemnly unto them, and shew them the manner of the king that shall reign over them." And Samuel told all the words of the LORD unto the people that asked of him a king. And he said, "This will be the manner of the king that shall reign over you: He will take your sons, and appoint them for himself, for his chariots, and to be his horsemen; and some shall run before his chariots. And he will appoint him captains over thousands, and captains over fifties; and will set them to ear his ground, and to reap his harvest, and to make his instruments of war, and instruments of his chariots. And he will take your daughters to be confectionaries, and to be cooks, and to be bakers. And he will take your fields, and your vineyards, and your oliveyards, even the best of them, and give them to his servants. And he will take the tenth of your seed, and of your vineyards, and give to his officers, and to his servants. And he will take your menservants, and your maidservants, and your goodliest young men, and your asses, and put them to his work. He will take the tenth of your sheep: and ye shall be his servants. And ye shall cry out in that day because of your king which ye shall have chosen you; and the LORD will not hear you in that day." Nevertheless the people refused to obey the voice of Samuel; and they said, "Nay; but we will have a king over us; that we also may be like all the nations; and that our king may judge us, and go out before us, and fight our battles." And Samuel heard all the words of the people, and he rehearsed them in the ears of the LORD. And the LORD said to Samuel, "Hearken unto their voice, and make them a king."

COMMENTARY: 1 Samuel 8:4-22 tells the story about when the elders of Israel told Samuel that the people wanted a king "like all other nations." God told Samuel to warn them how much a king would take i.e. their sons, daughters, fields, vineyards, menservants, maidservants, best young men, and taxes. In other words, God was not just warning them about the king. He was warning them about having a government that would demand so much from them. The Israelites would also have less freedom to spend their own money as they chose, because a greater portion of their income would be taken from them to pay taxes to support the government. Taxes would be 10%, the exact same amount due in tithes to God.

SCRIPTURE: Genesis 4:9 **(KJV):** "And the LORD said unto Cain, Where is Abel thy brother? And he said, I know not: Am I my brother's keeper?"

COMMENTARY: These are not words used by Christ, but words used by Cain immediately after he killed his brother Abel. They have absolutely nothing to do with the role of government.

SCRIPTURE: Matthew 22:37-40 **(KJV):**

81

Jesus said unto him, "Thou shalt love the Lord thy God with all thy heart, and with all thy soul, and with all thy mind. This is the first and great commandment. And the second is like unto it, Thou shalt love thy neighbour as thyself. On these two commandments hang all the law and the prophets."

COMMENTARY: Christ declared the second greatest commandment to be, "Thou shalt love thy neighbour as thyself." During the 2008 election, Senator Obama probably intended to refer to this concept, the duty to love one's fellow man as oneself, when he used the words, "I am my brother's keeper." However, he completely failed to understand that this is a command given by God to individuals and does not describe the purpose of government or grant any authority to government. More specifically, it does not give government authority to take money by force from those who have lawfully earned that money and give it to the poor in the form of benefits. That is not love. Love is by definition an act of the will. Christ's command gives individuals a duty to love one's fellow man as oneself, and this is an act of the will of the individual who chooses to be obedient to the command and to love his fellow man as he loves himself.

SCRIPTURE: Exodus 23:1-3 (TNIV): "Do not show favoritism to the poor in a lawsuit."[99]

COMMENTARY: Exodus 23:3 states that the government must ensure equal justice for the rich and the poor, and this also means it should not make judgments in favor of

---

[99] Holy Bible, Today's New International Version, 2001, 2005, International Bible Society.

the poor just because they are poor. The government should show impartiality not partiality toward the poor, because the government does not have authority, responsibility, or jurisdiction to favor or care for the poor.

SCRIPTURE: Leviticus 19:15 (KJV): "Ye shall do no unrighteousness in judgment: thou shalt not respect the person of the poor, nor honor the person of the mighty: but in righteousness shalt thou judge thy neighbour."

COMMENTARY: Leviticus 19 contains laws, which God directed Moses to give to the Israelites. Leviticus 19:15 states that one should not "respect" (favor) the poor in judgments. In other words, this verse also states that the government must ensure equal justice for the poor, and not make judgments in favor of the poor. Government should show impartiality not partiality toward the poor, because the government does not have authority, responsibility, or jurisdiction to favor or care for the poor.

SCRIPTURE: Romans 13:1-7 (New KJV):

Let every soul be subject to the governing authorities. For there is no authority except from God, and the authorities that exist are appointed by God. Therefore whoever resists the authority resists the ordinance of God, and those who resist will bring judgment on themselves. For rulers are not a terror to good works, but to evil. Do you want to be unafraid of the authority? Do what is good, and you will have praise from the same. For he is God's minister to you for good. But if you do evil, be afraid; for he does not bear the sword in vain;

for he is God's minister, an avenger to execute
wrath on him who practices evil. Therefore you
must be subject, not only because of wrath but
also for conscience' sake. For because of this
you also pay taxes, for they are God's ministers
attending continually to this very thing. Render
therefore to all their due: taxes to whom taxes
are due, customs to whom customs, fear to
whom fear, honor to whom honor.

COMMENTARY: Romans 13:1-7 is one of the most
important passages in Scripture about government. First, Paul
states the command that everyone must "be subject to the
governing authorities." Second, he states the reasons for this
command, that "there is no authority except from God" and
that all "authorities that exist are appointed by God." Third, he
draws a conclusion based upon this rule, that anyone who
resists authority resists God's law and "bring[s] judgment on
themselves." This general rule and conclusion apply to "all
authorities that exist" (parents, employers, etc.), but Paul's
concentration in this passage is on government authorities.
Fourth, Paul states that Rulers are "God's ministers" for good,
but they do "not bear the sword in vain" because they are
God's "avenger to execute wrath" on those who do evil. Fifth,
Paul concludes that one must be subject to government
authorities, not just for fear of their "wrath," but for
"conscience' sake" (because it is the right thing to do). Sixth,
Paul makes one final conclusion, that one should therefore give
taxes, customs, fear, and honor to the authorities as is due to
them.

All authorities are "appointed by God" and are "God's
ministers." If God wants everyone to fear and honor
government authorities, then what does God think about how

some Americans treat elected officials? Governor Clinton won a presidential election with the phrase, "It's the economy, stupid." The word stupid was used to belittle the first President Bush, a man of great honor and dignity. Many Democrats, talk show hosts, and others mocked the second President Bush, in complete disobedience to this Scriptural directive.

CONCLUSION. Scripture discusses the role of government. Romans 13:1-7 states that all "authorities that exist are appointed by God," and that anyone who resists the authorities resists God's law and brings "judgment on themselves." Rulers are "God's ministers" for good. They do "not bear the sword in vain" because they are God's "avenger to execute wrath" on evildoers. One must be subject to government authorities not just for fear of their "wrath," but because it is the right thing to do. All citizens must pay taxes and give proper respect to government officials.

During the 2008 election, Senator Obama often quoted the words "I am my brother's keeper" to explain what motivates him to government service. However, these are not words used by Christ, but words used by Cain after killing his brother Abel (Gen. 4:9). They have nothing to do with government.

Exactly what part of Scripture gives government any responsibility or authority to care for the poor or the middle class or anyone else? Answer: No part. In "Matthew 22:37-40 Christ gives the command to "love thy neighbor as thyself." This commandment is given to individuals; it does not grant any authority to government. Obedience requires a very personal act of the will of the individual who chooses to love his neighbor. The purpose of government is not to provide or care for citizens, but to protect life and liberty and thereby enable the pursuit of happiness.

Exodus 23:3 and Leviticus 19:15 both direct government to ensure equal justice for the poor, and not make judgments in favor of the poor. Government should show impartiality not partiality toward the poor, because the government does not have authority, responsibility, or jurisdiction to favor the poor.

In 1 Samuel 8:8-20 God told Samuel to warn the people that a king would take their sons, daughters, fields, vineyards, menservants, maidservants, best young men, and 10% in taxes, the same amount due in tithes to God. God clearly recommends the smallest possible government, which gives the people the greatest possible freedom to keep and spend their own earnings. The founding fathers of the United States understood God's ideal, which is embodied in the U.S. Constitution, of smaller government, lower taxes, and greater personal freedom and responsibility for all citizens. They were fiercely independent men who greatly treasured their freedom and would not trade it for government benefits.

CHAPTER 5.2

SCRIPTURE ON TAXES

INTRODUCTION. Again, "fairness" in taxation is one of the primary themes of Democrats. Democrats always claim that the "wealthy few" do not pay their fair share of taxes and that the middle class pay more than their fair share. The chapter on Truth in Taxes proved this totally false, showing that about half of Americans, mostly middle and lower class, do not pay any federal taxes, and that the rich pay much higher taxes than the poor or middle class. So what is the heart and mind of God on taxes? Does Scripture give any hint about where God stands on this hot political issue?

SCRIPTURE. This chapter looks at two Old Testament passages. First, consider God's command through Moses in Leviticus:

> And all the tithe of the land, whether of the seed of the land, or of the fruit of the tree, is the Lord's: it is holy unto the Lord. And if a man will at all redeem ought of his tithes, he shall add thereto the fifth part thereof. And concerning the tithe of the herd, or of the flock, even of whatsoever passeth under the rod, the tenth shall be holy unto the Lord (Leviticus 27:30-32).

Note that the God's tithe or "tax rate" was a tenth (10%) for everyone, both the rich and the poor. See also Deut. 12:5-11; 14:22-28; Num. 18:24-28; Mal. 3:8-10; Heb. 7:1-4.

Second, consider 1 Samuel 8:8-20. See prior chapter for more complete quote (1 Samuel 8:4-22).

And Samuel told all the words of the LORD unto the people that asked of him a king. And he said, "This will be the manner of the king that shall reign over you: He will take your sons, and appoint them for himself, for his chariots, and to be his horsemen; and some shall run before his chariots. And he will appoint him captains over thousands, and captains over fifties; and will set them to ear his ground, and to reap his harvest, and to make his instruments of war, and instruments of his chariots. And he will take your daughters to be confectionaries, and to be cooks, and to be bakers. And he will take your fields, and your vineyards, and your oliveyards, even the best of them, and give them to his servants. And he will take the tenth of your seed, and of your vineyards, and give to his officers, and to his servants. And he will take your menservants, and your maidservants, and your goodliest young men, and your asses, and put them to his work. He will take the tenth of your sheep: and ye shall be his servants. And ye shall cry out in that day because of your king which ye shall have chosen you; and the LORD will not hear you in that day."

Note that God tells Samuel to warn the people that a king would take their sons, daughters, fields, vineyards, menservants, maidservants, best young men, and taxes. Taxes would be 10%, the same amount due in tithes to God.

CONCLUSION.   So where does God stand on taxes for the rich and the poor? First, God's "tax rate" for tithes is exactly the same rate for the rich and the poor: 10%. Second, God warned that a king would charge exactly the same rate for the rich and the poor: 10%. Thus it would seem that in the eyes of God a flat tax rate that is exactly the same for both the rich and the poor would be the "fairest" rate.

God warned the Israelites about the heavy burden that a king would impose, when the tax rate would be only 10%, which is far less than most Americans pay today. It seems quite clear from a careful reading of 1 Samuel 8:8-20 that God would strongly recommend the smallest possible federal government as envisioned by the founding fathers of our nation and as required by the highest law of the land, the Constitution.

What does scripture say about different treatment of different economic classes? Exodus 23:3 and Leviticus 19:15, quoted in the prior chapter, direct government to ensure equal justice for the poor, and not make judgments in favor of the poor. In other words, government should show impartiality not partiality toward the poor, because the government does not have authority, responsibility, or jurisdiction to favor the poor.

CHAPTER 5.3

SCRIPTURE ON ABORTION

INTRODUCTION. Life is the first, most basic, most fundamental, most important inalienable right mentioned in the Declaration of Independence. Without life, all other rights are meaningless, because no one can exercise any rights without life.

A candidate's position on abortion should be a deciding factor for Christians. Scripture reveals the heart and mind of God and His laws, which are rooted in His unchanging character. A candidate's position on abortion reveals the heart and mind of the candidate in relation to the heart and mind of God and His laws.

Is abortion a woman's right to choose to control her own body, or is it murder of an innocent, completely helpless child? Most Republicans are pro-life. They believe abortion is murder of an innocent, completely helpless child. Most Democrats are pro-abortion. They believe that a woman believes a woman has a right to terminate the life of her unborn child before birth. See Congressional voting scorecards.

Most Democrats in Congress voted to support all pro-abortion policies supported by President Obama, except the after-birth killing of a child that survives abortion. When Democrats have a majority in Congress, they chair the Senate Judiciary Committee and block the nomination of pro-life Christian judges to the Supreme Court and Federal Courts.

What does Scripture say about the heart and mind of God on abortion? Scripture provides answers through the words of Abraham, Moses, King David, Job, Isaiah, Jeremiah, Luke, the Apostle Paul, and other authors of Scripture.

SCRIPTURE: Exodus 21:22-23 (KJV):

"If men strive, and hurt a woman with child, so that her fruit depart from her, and yet no mischief follow: he shall surely be punished, according as the woman's husband will lay upon him; and he shall pay as the judges determine. And if any mischief follow, then thou shall give him life for life."

COMMENTARY: In Exodus 21:22-23 God speaks to Moses, giving His law regarding death of an unborn child, revealing His heart and mind on abortion. If there is no "mischief" and the death of the unborn child is purely an accident, then the man who caused the unborn child's death is fined as determined by the husband and judge. However, if "mischief" is involved, then the penalty for killing the unborn child is the death penalty. The value of the life of the unborn child is the same as the value of the man guilty of the "mischief," hence the penalty of "life for life." In this passage God makes it perfectly clear that the penalty for deliberate killing an unborn child should be the death penalty. This does not mean that God would want us to impose the death penalty on anyone guilty of abortion. It does mean that we should change our laws to outlaw abortion. Cases involving the life of the mother pose a separate moral issue.

The Hebrew word for the unborn child in Ex. 21:22 is used throughout the Old Testament to refer to children before and after birth ("hareh," word 2030, Strong's Exhaustive Concordance of the Bible, James Strong, Ed.). See Gen. 16:11; 17:10,12,14; 19:36; 38:24,25; Ex. 21:22; 22:22; Lev. 12:2,5; 1 Sam. 4:19; 2 Sam. 11:5; 2Kin. 8:12; 15:16; Isa. 26:17,18; 49:15; 54:1; Jer. 31:8; Hos. 13:16; Am. 1:13. In other words, a child is a child, a human life, before and after birth.

SCRIPTURE: Psalm 127:3 (KJV): "Lo, children are an heritage of the LORD: and the fruit of the womb is his reward."

Deuteronomy 7:12-13 (KJV):

"Wherefore it shall come to pass, if ye hearken to these judgments, and keep, and do them, that the LORD thy God shall keep unto thee the covenant and the mercy which he sware unto thy fathers: And he will love thee, and bless thee, and multiply thee: he will also bless the fruit of thy womb, and the fruit of thy land, thy corn, and thy wine, and thine oil, the increase of thy kine, and the flocks of thy sheep, in the land which he sware unto thy fathers to give thee."

COMMENTARY: Psalm 127:3 states that children, the "fruit of the womb," are a "reward" and "heritage of the LORD." Deuteronomy 7:12-13 shows that one of God's blessings upon His people if they are obedient to his commandments is the "fruit of thy womb," the gift of having children. All children are a blessing from God, and with the blessing comes responsibility for proper care of the child, before and after birth.

SCRIPTURE: Psalm 139:13-16 (NKJV): 100

"For You formed my inward parts; You covered me in my mother's womb. I will praise You, for I am fearfully *and* wonderfully made; marvelous are Your works, and *that* my soul knows very well. My frame was not hidden from You, when I was made in secret, *and* skillfully wrought in the lowest parts of the earth. Your eyes saw my substance, being yet unformed, and in Your book they all were written, the days fashioned for me, when *as yet there were* none of them."

Job 31:15 (KJV): "Did not he that made me in the womb make him? And did not one fashion us in the womb?"

Isaiah 44:2 (KJV): "The LORD that made thee, and formed thee from the womb, which will help thee…."

Isaiah 44:24 (KJV): "The LORD…that formed thee from the womb, I am the LORD that maketh all things; that stretcheth forth the heavens alone; that spreadeth abroad the earth by myself…."

Isaiah 49:1,5 (KJV): "The LORD hath called me from the womb…. And now, saith the LORD that formed me from the womb to be his servant, to bring Jacob again to him …."

Jeremiah 1:5 (KJV): "Before I formed thee in the belly I knew thee; and before thou camest forth out of the womb I sanctified thee, and I ordained thee a prophet unto the nations."

COMMENTARY: These verses affirm that God forms each person within the womb. Psalm 139:13-16, written by King David, is one of the most beautiful passages in the Bible. It states, "You formed my inward parts…I am fearfully *and*

---

[100] Holy Bible, New King James Version, 1982, Thomas Nelson, Inc.

wonderfully made.... I was made in secret, *and* skillfully wrought." These words imply that every person is formed by God within the womb, "fearfully and wonderfully made...skillfully wrought." Then David states that God "saw my substance, being yet unformed, and in Your book they all were written, the days fashioned for me, when *as yet there were* none of them." These words tell us that God sees every day of everyone's life before He forms them in the womb.

Job 31:15 uses the words "fashion us in the womb." Isaiah 49:5 states that God "formed" Isaiah "to be his servant, to bring Jacob" (Israel) back to him. Jeremiah 1:5 states that God "knew" Jeremiah before He formed him in the womb, and "sanctified" and "ordained" him to be "a prophet unto the nations." These passages inform us that God forms each person in the womb and that he creates people with a purpose, to serve Him.

The Declaration of Independence affirms that God creates "all men" and endows them with the right to life, describing these as "self-evident" truths. "We hold these truths to be self-evident, that all men are created equal, that they are endowed by their Creator with certain unalienable Rights, that among these are Life, Liberty and the pursuit of Happiness."

SCRIPTURE: Luke 1:13-15 (KJV):

"But the angel said unto him, Fear not,
Zacharias: for thy prayer is heard; and thy wife
Elisabeth shall bear thee a son, and thou shalt
call his name John. And thou shalt have joy and
gladness; and many shall rejoice at his birth.
For he shall be great in the sight of the Lord,
and shall drink neither wine nor strong drink;

and he shall be filled with the Holy Ghost, even
from his mother's womb."

Luke 1:30-31 (KJV): "And the angel said unto her,
Fear not, Mary: for thou hast found favour with God. And,
behold, thou shalt conceive in thy womb, and bring forth a son,
and shalt call his name JESUS."

COMMENTARY: These passages contain prophecy of
angels about the conception and birth of Jesus and John the
Baptist. In Luke 1:13-15 the angel states that John will be
filled with the Spirit of God before birth, within his mother's
womb. In Luke 1:30-31 the angel tells Mary that she will
conceive and give birth to Jesus. These passages show that
God controls conception and birth, and that he forms a person
within the womb for a purpose. Luke 1:13-15 also raises the
question: How could anyone kill a child who could be filled
the Spirit of God in the womb?

SCRIPTURE: Luke 1:41-44 (KJV):

"And it came to pass, that, when Elisabeth
heard the salutation of Mary, the babe leaped in
her womb; and Elisabeth was filled with the
Holy Ghost: And she spake out with a loud
voice, and said, Blessed art thou among women,
and blessed is the fruit of thy womb. And
whence is this to me, that the mother of my
Lord should come to me? For, lo, as soon as the
voice of thy salutation sounded in mine ears, the
babe leaped in my womb for joy."

Luke 18:15-16 (KJV): "And they brought unto him also
infants, that he would touch them: but when his disciples saw

it, they rebuked them. But Jesus called them unto him, and said, 'Suffer little children to come unto me, and forbid them not: for of such is the kingdom of God.'"

COMMENTARY: Luke 1:41-44 is the story of the meeting of Mary, when she was pregnant with Jesus, with Elisabeth, when she was pregnant with John the Baptist. John the Baptist "leaped...for joy" within his mother's womb when he heard the voice of the mother of Jesus. How can anyone abort a child that is able to recognize the voice of the mother of Jesus and jump for joy within his mother's womb?

The Greek word for the unborn child in Luke 1:41-44 is used in the New Testament to refer to children before and after birth ("brephos" word 1025, The Word Study Concordance, George Wigram and Ralph Winter, Ed. 1972 & 1978. It is used to refer to baby Jesus wrapped in swaddling clothes (Luke 2:12) and lying in a manger (Luke 2:16), the little children (infants) brought to Jesus (Luke 18:15), young children (Acts 7:19), a young child (2 Tim 3:15), and newborn babies (1 Pet. 2:2). In other words, a child is a child before and after birth.

SCRIPTURE: Genesis 18:10-15 (KJV):

And he said, I will certainly return unto thee according to the time of life; and, lo, Sarah thy wife shall have a son. And Sarah heard it in the tent door, which was behind him. Now Abraham and Sarah were old and well stricken in age; and it ceased to be with Sarah after the manner of women. Therefore Sarah laughed within herself, saying, "After I am waxed old shall I have pleasure, my lord being old also?" And the LORD said unto Abraham, Wherefore

96

did Sarah laugh, saying, Shall I of a surety bear a child, which am old? Is any thing too hard for the LORD? At the time appointed I will return unto thee, according to the time of life, and Sarah shall have a son. Then Sarah denied, saying, I laughed not; for she was afraid. And he said, "Nay; but thou didst laugh."

Romans 4:19 (KJV): "And being not weak in faith, he considered not his own body now dead, when he was about an hundred years old, neither yet the deadness of Sarah's womb."

COMMENTARY: Genesis 18:10-15 and Romans 4:19 are about Abraham and Sarah. The key words in Genesis 18:10-15 are: "Is any thing too hard for the LORD?" God made Sarah, who was very old and no longer able to have children, conceive and bear a child, to fulfill His promise to give Abraham many descendents. Note that Sarah "laughed within herself", but the LORD who sees the heart and mind knew that she had laughed. Romans 4:19 is about Abraham faith that he would have a child with Sarah as promised by God, even though he was about a hundred years old and his wife was barren. This passage shows that God is able to miraculously cause conception and birth regardless of the age or physical condition of the father or mother.

DECLARATION OF INDEPENDENCE. The Declaration of Independence is a pro-life document. First, it affirms that all men have a god-given right to life. Second, it affirms that all men are created equal. In other words, from conception until birth God creates each person in his or her mother's womb, and makes that person equal in value to all other persons.

Voting with the Declaration of Independence requires voting Republican because it is a pro-life document.

CONCLUSION. God makes his position on abortion clear through scripture. In Exodus 21:22-23 God tells Moses that the penalty for the deliberate killing of an unborn child is the death penalty. This does not mean that God would want us to assume jurisdiction to impose the death penalty on everyone one guilty of abortion. However, it does mean that they are nevertheless deserving of death under God's laws and that we should therefore change our laws to outlaw abortion. Cases involving the life of the mother pose a separate moral issue, but that does not justify using "life of the mother" as an excuse for the murder of unborn children.

The Declaration of Independence affirms that God creates "all men" and endows them with certain God-given inalienable rights, which include the right to life. The right to life begins at conception, not birth. A mother's duty to care for her child begins at conception, not birth. A mother who abuses that right of her child by using drugs or alcohol during pregnancy endangers the health of her child.

The founding fathers of the United States understood that the "self-evident" truths and "inalienable rights" cited in the Declaration of Independence were common-sense teachings of Scripture. Job 31:15; Isaiah 44:2; 44:24; 49:5 **and Jeremiah 1:5** affirm that God forms each person within the womb. In Psalm 139:13-16 King David teaches that everyone is "formed" and "fearfully and wonderfully made" and "skillfully wrought" by God within the womb, and that God sees every day of a person's life before He forms him or her in the womb. Genesis 18:10-15 and Romans 4:19 show that God is able to cause conception and birth regardless of the age of the father and mother. Psalm 127:3 and Deuteronomy 7:12-13 teach that children are a blessing from the Lord. That blessing brings responsibility for proper care of the child, before and after birth.

Luke 1:13-15; 30-31 prophesizes the conception and birth of Jesus and John the Baptist, showing that God controls conception and birth and forms a person within the womb for a purpose. Luke 1:13-15 and 1:41-44 raise the question: How could anyone kill an unborn child who is filled the Spirit of God and be able to recognize the voice of the mother of Jesus and jump for joy within the womb?

The Hebrew word used in the Old Testament and the Greek word used in the New Testament to refer to unborn children are the same words used to refer to children after birth. In other words, a child is a child before and after birth, as precious as baby Jesus lying in a manger (Luke 2:12,16) and the little children brought to Jesus (Luke 18:15-16).

Many ancient cultures practiced child sacrifice. Most Americans cannot begin to understand how any people could be so cruel and evil to sacrifice children on stone alters to secure the blessings of their false gods. If any group of Americans sacrificed a child on an altar today, most Americans would be horrified and demand the death penalty. Abortion is child sacrifice. In the world today, unwanted children are sacrificed on the alter of convenience by an ungodly, godless people who do whatever is right in their own eyes and seek first not to love and serve God but to serve themselves.

Scripture reveals the heart and mind of God and His laws, which are rooted in His unchanging character. A candidate's stand on abortion speaks volumes about them; it reveals their heart and mind and the condition of their moral compass. Comparing a candidate's position on abortion with Scripture reveals whether or not the candidate's heart and mind are in sync with God and His laws, or whether the candidate simply does whatever is right in his own eyes. Every American who votes for any Democrat has the blood of American children on his hands.

CHAPTER 5.4

SCRIPTURE ON HOMOSEXUALITY AND SAME-SEX MARRIAGE

INTRODUCTION. This chapter tackles homosexuality and same-sex marriage because a candidate's position on these issues should be a deciding factor for Christians. Homosexuals include Lesbians, Gays, Bisexuals, and Transvestites (LGBT). Scripture very clearly reveals the heart and mind of God and His laws on homosexuality, laws rooted in His unchanging character. A candidate's position on these topics clearly reveals the heart and mind of the candidate in relation to the heart and mind of God and His laws.

Democrats are far more supportive of homosexuality and same-sex marriage than Republicans. This can be quickly proven by reference to the voting records of members of Congress.[101] Most Christian leaders remain silent, detached from reality, irrelevant, failures not only at providing moral leadership, but also at making it clear what it means to be a Christian.

Scripture reveals the heart and mind of God on homosexuality and same-sex marriage through the story of creation in Genesis, laws of God given through Moses in Leviticus, and letters from the Apostle Paul to Timothy and to the Romans and Corinthians.

SCRIPTURE: Genesis 2:18-24 (KJV):

---

[101] "Vote Scorecard," Family Research Council Action, http://www.frcaction.org (accessed July 9, 2008).

And the LORD God said, It is not good that the man should be alone; I will make him an help meet for him. And out of the ground the LORD God formed every beast of the field, and every fowl of the air; and brought them unto Adam to see what he would call them: and whatsoever Adam called every living creature, that was the name thereof. And Adam gave names to all cattle, and to the fowl of the air, and to every beast of the field; but for Adam there was not found an help meet for him. And the LORD God caused a deep sleep to fall upon Adam, and he slept: and he took one of his ribs, and closed up the flesh instead thereof; And the rib, which the LORD God had taken from man, made he a woman, and brought her unto the man. And Adam said, This is now bone of my bones, and flesh of my flesh: she shall be called Woman, because she was taken out of Man. Therefore shall a man leave his father and his mother, and shall cleave unto his wife: and they shall be one flesh."

COMMENTARY: Genesis 2:18-24 is the story of God's creation of man, then woman from man to be a suitable companion for man, and finally marriage as a special union between one man and one woman wherein "they shall be one flesh." Note that God created woman very different from man, to make her a suitable companion for man. Another man would not be a suitable companion. Note that in God's design for marriage, the man leaves his father and mother (his family), to form a special "one flesh" union with his wife, which we call marriage, and to start a new family. The new marriage couple is then responsible to be obedient to the dominion mandate to "be fruitful and multiply," which is impossible in a same-sex marriage.

SCRIPTURE: Leviticus 18:22-26 (KJV):

"Thou shalt not lie with mankind, as with womankind: it is abomination. Neither shalt thou lie with any beast to defile thyself therewith: neither shall any woman stand before a beast to lie down thereto: it is confusion. Defile not ye yourselves in any of these things: for in all these the nations are defiled which I cast out before you: And the land is defiled: therefore I do visit the iniquity thereof upon it, and the land itself vomiteth out her inhabitants. Ye shall therefore keep my statutes and my judgments, and shall not commit any of these abominations; neither any of your own nation, nor any stranger that sojourneth among you."

COMMENTARY: In Leviticus 18:22-26 Moses recites commandments directly from God to the Israelites. God commands that men not have sexual relations with other men or beasts because is an "abomination." He states that it defiles the men who do it and their nations. God punishes a nation defiled by these sins. God warns the Israelites to keep His statutes and judgments, to not commit these abominations, and to not even allow a stranger who lives among them to "commit any of these abominations." The word "abomination" is used to describe something that is extremely offensive to God, an extreme perversion of His design and law.

SCRIPTURE: Leviticus 20:13-16 (KJV):

"If a man also lie with mankind, as he lieth with a woman, both of them have committed an abomination: they shall surely be put to death; their blood shall be upon them. And if a man take a wife and her mother, it is wickedness: they shall be burnt with fire, both he and they; that there be no wickedness among you. And if a man lie with a beast, he shall surely be put to death: and ye shall slay the beast. And if a woman approach unto any beast, and lie down thereto, thou shalt kill the woman, and the beast: they shall surely be put to death; their blood shall be upon them."

COMMENTARY: In Leviticus 20:13-16 God states His law regarding two men having sex. God declares it is an "abomination" (extreme perversion) which must be punished by death. The same penalty applies to a man who has sex with his wife and her mother and to a man or woman who has sex with an animal. This does not mean that we should impose the death penalty for sodomy. It does mean we should not support candidates who are so strongly opposed to God and His laws.

SCRIPTURE: Romans 1:16-32 (KJV):

For I am not ashamed of the gospel of Christ: for it is the power of God unto salvation to every one that believeth; to the Jew first, and also to the Greek. For therein is the righteousness of God revealed from faith to faith: as it is written, The just shall live by faith. For the wrath of God is revealed from heaven against all ungodliness and unrighteousness of men, who hold the truth in unrighteousness; Because that which may be known of God is manifest in them; for God hath shewed it unto them. For the invisible things of him from the creation of the world are clearly seen, being understood by the things that are made, even his eternal power and Godhead; so that they are without excuse: Because that, when they knew God, they glorified him not as God, neither were thankful; but became vain in their imaginations, and their foolish heart was darkened. Professing themselves to be wise, they became fools, And changed the glory of the uncorruptible God into an image made like to corruptible man, and to birds, and fourfooted beasts, and creeping things. Wherefore God also gave them up to uncleanness through the lusts of their own hearts, to dishonour their own bodies between themselves: Who changed the truth of God into a lie, and worshipped and served the creature more than the Creator, who is blessed for ever. Amen. For this cause God gave them up unto vile affections: for even their women did change the natural use into that which is against nature: And likewise also the men, leaving the natural use of the woman, burned in their lust one toward another; men with men working that which is unseemly, and receiving in themselves that recompence of their error which was meet. And even as they did not like to retain God in their knowledge, God gave them over to a reprobate mind, to do those things which are not convenient; Being filled with all unrighteousness, fornication, wickedness, covetousness, maliciousness; full of envy, murder, debate, deceit, malignity; whisperers, Backbiters, haters of God, despiteful, proud, boasters, inventors of evil things, disobedient to parents, Without understanding, covenantbreakers, without natural affection, implacable, unmerciful: Who knowing the judgment of God, that they which commit such things are worthy of death, not only do the same, but have pleasure in them that do them.

COMMENTARY: In Romans 1:16-32 Paul reveals the heart and mind of God on homosexuality and other ungodliness and unrighteousness. First, he states that God reveals His wrath against "all ungodliness and unrighteousness of men, who hold the truth in unrighteousness." Then he explains why men choose ungodliness and unrighteousness and suffer the wrath of God: (1) First, because they know what can be known about God because God has shown it to them. (2) Second, because the "invisible things" of God are "clearly seen" because they are understood from observing the things that God created. These "invisible things" of God that are "clearly seen" include His "eternal power and Godhead" so they are "without excuse." (3) Third, because although they knew God, they did not glorify Him as God and were not thankful, but became "vain in their imaginations" and their "foolish heart was darkened." Claiming to be wise, they became fools, and exchanged the glory of "uncorruptible God" for an image of "corruptible man," etc. Then Paul explains what God did to these ungodly, unrighteous fools: (1) First, He gave them up to their own lusts, to dishonor their bodies "between themselves" because they rejected the truth of

God for a lie, and "worshiped and served" God's creation more than the Creator. (2) Second, he gave them up to "vile affections." Women changed the "natural use" of their bodies for that "against nature." Men likewise rejected "natural use of the woman," "burned in their lust" for other men, and did "unseemly" things with other men. As a result they received due punishment for their wrongdoing. (3) Third, because they rejected God, He gave them up to a "reprobate mind," to do thing which are "not convenient." Then Paul lists the wrongdoing of these reprobate men and women: "all unrighteousness, fornication, wickedness, covetousness, maliciousness; full of envy, murder, debate, deceit, malignity; whisperers, backbiters, haters of God, despiteful, proud, boasters, inventors of evil things, disobedient to parents, without understanding, covenantbreakers, without natural affection, implacable, unmerciful." Finally, Paul ends by saying that they not only did all these evil things, but actually took pleasure in doing them, although they knew the "judgment of God" meant they were deserving of death for their wrongdoing."

SCRIPTURE: 1 Corinthians 6:9-10 (New KJV):

Do you not know that the unrighteous will not inherit the kingdom of God? Do not be deceived. Neither fornicators, nor idolaters, nor adulterers, nor homosexuals, nor sodomites, nor thieves, nor covetous, nor drunkards, nor revilers, nor extortioners will inherit the kingdom of God" (1 Cor. 6:9-10, NKJV). [102]

---

[102] Holy Bible, New King James Version, 1982, Thomas Nelson, Inc..

COMMENTARY: 1 Corinthians 6:9-10 states that the "unrighteous will not inherit the kingdom of God" and that this includes "homosexuals" and "sodomites."

SCRIPTURE: 1 Timothy 1:9-10 (NKJV):

Knowing this: that the law is not made for a righteous person, but for *the* lawless and insubordinate, for *the* ungodly and for sinners, for *the* unholy and profane, for murderers of fathers and murderers of mothers, for manslayers, for fornicators, for sodomites, for kidnappers, for liars, for perjurers, and if there is any other thing that is contrary to sound doctrine....

COMMENTARY: 1 Timothy 1:9-10 shows that God considers homosexuals who commit sodomy to be "lawless...insubordinate...ungodly...sinners...unholy and profane."

CONCLUSION. Scripture is very clear about marriage and homosexuality. God created man male and female, and marriage to be a special union between one man and one woman (Genesis 2:18-24). He designed the family as the most fundamental unit in society, critical to its stability and proper function. Homosexuality and same-sex marriage are extreme perversions of God's design for man, woman, sex, marriage, and family. Homosexual acts are abominations to God deserving of the death penalty. There is absolutely no way that any individual or nation can ignore God's design for sex, marriage, and family without severe consequences.

Homosexuals call those who oppose them "homophobic," berating them with totally false accusations of fear of homosexuals. The opposite may be true. They may rightfully have greater fear and respect for God than man, and rightfully feel some of the same disgust for the extreme sexual perversion of homosexuality that God feels toward those who have so greatly perverted his design for man, woman, marriage, and family. Friends of the homosexual movement demonstrate greater fear of man than God, extreme ignorance, and extreme foolishness.

A candidate's positions on same-sex marriage and homosexuality should be deciding factors in voting because these sins are extremely offensive to God and because this subject area is so critically important to the future of our nation. Democrats are far more supportive of the homosexual lifestyle and same-sex marriage than Republicans. See Vote Scorecards of Family Research Council Action and Family Alliance. Any American who votes for any Democrat or in any way helps Democrats gain control of the Presidency, Congress or any other political office will answer to God for supporting a lifestyle which is an extreme perversion of God's design for man, woman, and marriage.

CHAPTER 6.0

VOTING CONSTITUTION AND DECLARATION OF INDEPENDENCE

SECTION REVIEW. This section shows what voting in accordance with principles and laws embodied in the Declaration of Independence, Constitution, and Bill of Rights requires. Chapter 7.1 discusses the Declaration of Independence. Chapter 7.2 discusses the Constitution. Chapter 7.3 discusses the Bill of Rights.

CHAPTERS:
6.1 Voting Declaration of Independence
6.2 Voting Constitution
6.3 Voting Bill of Rights

CHAPTER 6.1

VOTING DECLARATION OF INDEPENDENCE

INTRODUCTION. This chapter addresses basic principles embodied in the Declaration of Independence. First, it discusses the "most important principle" that the United States was founded upon. Second, it reviews the very long list of "causes for separation" from Great Britain. Third, it briefly mentions efforts to resolve problems with Great Britain. Fourth, it reviews the final section, the actual declaration of independence from Great Britain. Finally, it discusses rights cited within the Declaration of Independence i.e. the rights to life, liberty, pursuit of happiness, and the right to bear arms. See Appendixes for full text of Declaration of Independence.

FOUNDING PRINCIPLE OF UNITED STATES. What is the most important principle that the United States was founded upon? Now let me rephrase the question to further clarify exactly what I am asking. What is the most important, most fundamental, most irreplaceable principle that the United States was founded upon? Answer: The United States was founded upon the principle that: (1) God created all things seen and unseen and all laws that govern all things seen and unseen; (2) God creates all men equal with "certain unalienable Rights," (3) "to secure these rights, governments are instituted," (4) "whenever any…government becomes destructive of these ends, it is the Right of the People to alter or to abolish it, and to institute new government;" (5) this new government must be established in accordance with God's laws to protect the God-given unalienable rights of all men.[103]

---

[103] "Declaration of Independence," U.S. National Archives & Records Administration. http://www.archives.gov/exhibits/charters/declaration.html.

This most important, most fundamental, most irreplaceable principle that the United States was founded upon is partially stated and partially implied in the Declaration of Independence.

> We hold these truths to be self-evident, that all men are created equal, that they are endowed by their Creator with certain unalienable Rights, that among these are Life, Liberty and the pursuit of Happiness.--That to secure these rights, Governments are instituted among Men, deriving their just powers from the consent of the governed, --That whenever any Form of Government becomes destructive of these ends, it is the Right of the People to alter or to abolish it, and to institute new Government, laying its foundation on such principles and organizing its powers in such form, as to them shall seem most likely to effect their Safety and Happiness.[104]

CAUSES FOR SEPARATION. The first sentence of the Declaration of Independence announces its purpose: to "declare the causes which impel them to the separation" from Great Britain. It cites, as justification, the "Laws of nature and Nature's God."[105]

> When in the Course of human events, it becomes necessary for one people to dissolve the political bands which have connected them with another, and to assume among the powers

---

[104] Ibid.
[105] Ibid.

of the earth, the separate and equal station to which the Laws of Nature and of Nature's God entitle them, a decent respect to the opinions of mankind requires that they should declare the causes which impel them to the separation.[i]

The founding fathers understood that: (1) God created all things seen and unseen and all laws that govern all things seen and unseen; (2) these laws justified the Declaration of Independence from Great Britain; and (3) these laws were the legal foundation for the establishment of a new, independent nation.

The first cause for separation cited refers to God as the Creator who continues to create all men equal. This belief is based upon Scripture. God told the prophet Jeremiah: "Before I formed thee in the belly I knew thee; and before thou [came] forth out of the womb I sanctified thee, and I ordained thee a prophet unto the nations" (Jer. 1:5, KJV). Job said, "Did not he that made me in the womb make him? and did not one fashion us in the womb?" (Job 31:15, KJV). King David said, "I will praise thee; for I am fearfully and wonderfully made: marvelous are thy works; and that my soul know[s] right well. My substance was not hid from thee, when I was made in secret, and curiously wrought in the lowest parts of the earth. Thine eyes did see my substance, yet being unperfected; and in thy book all my members were written, which in continuance were fashioned, when as yet there was none of them" (Ps. 139: 14-16, KJV). See also Beck. 11:5; Isa. 44:2, 24; 49:1-5; Jer. 1:5; Luke 1:15,41-44.

The first cause for separation then states that God gives every man "certain unalienable Rights, that among these are

Life, Liberty and the pursuit of Happiness."[106] It states "that to secure these rights, Governments are instituted among Men, deriving their just powers from the consent of the governed" and "that whenever any Form of Government becomes destructive of these ends, it is the Right of the People to alter or to abolish it, and to institute new Government, laying its foundation on such principles and organizing its powers in such form, as to them shall seem most likely to effect their Safety and Happiness."[107] "Unalienable Rights" are God-given rights which no man or government has the right to take away from any man. It is the violation of these rights, which God gives to every man, that justify the Declaration of Independence from Great Britain and the formation of a new government.

The Declaration states that "Governments long established should not be changed for light and transient causes" but when there is a "long train of abuses and usurpations…it is their right, it is their duty, to throw off such Government, and to provide new Guards for their future security."[108] These "new Guards" are the protections embodied in the U.S. Constitution.

The next section of the Declaration of Independence gives an incredibly long list of the "repeated injuries and usurpations" of the "King of Great Britain…all having in direct object the establishment of an absolute Tyranny over these States."[109] These abuses justified the Declaration of Independence from Great Britain.

---

[106] Ibid.
[107] Ibid.
[108] Ibid.
[109] Ibid.

He has refused his Assent to Laws, the most wholesome and necessary for the public good.
He has forbidden his Governors to pass Laws of immediate and pressing importance, unless suspended in their operation till his Assent should be obtained; and when so suspended, he has utterly neglected to attend to them.
He has refused to pass other Laws for the accommodation of large districts of people, unless those people would relinquish the right of Representation in the Legislature, a right inestimable to them and formidable to tyrants only.
He has called together legislative bodies at places unusual, uncomfortable, and distant from the depository of their public Records, for the sole purpose of fatiguing them into compliance with his measures.
He has dissolved Representative Houses repeatedly, for opposing with manly firmness his invasions on the rights of the people.
He has refused for a long time, after such dissolutions, to cause others to be elected; whereby the Legislative powers, incapable of Annihilation, have returned to the People at large for their exercise; the State remaining in the mean time exposed to all the dangers of invasion from without, and convulsions within.
He has [endeavored] to prevent the population of these States; for that purpose obstructing the Laws for Naturalization of Foreigners; refusing to pass others to encourage their migrations hither, and raising the conditions of new Appropriations of Lands.
He has obstructed the Administration of Justice, by refusing his Assent to Laws for establishing Judiciary powers.
He has made Judges dependent on his Will alone,

for the tenure of their offices, and the amount and payment of their salaries.

He has erected a multitude of New Offices, and sent hither swarms of Officers to harass our people, and eat out their substance.

He has kept among us, in times of peace, Standing Armies without the Consent of our legislatures.

He has affected to render the Military independent of and superior to the Civil power.

He has combined with others to subject us to a jurisdiction foreign to our constitution, and unacknowledged by our laws; giving his Assent to their Acts of pretended Legislation:

For Quartering large bodies of armed troops among us:

For protecting them, by a mock Trial, from punishment for any Murders which they should commit on the Inhabitants of these States:

For cutting off our Trade with all parts of the world:

For **imposing Taxes on us without our Consent**:

For depriving us in many cases, of the benefits of Trial by Jury:

For transporting us beyond Seas to be tried for pretended offences

For abolishing the free System of English Laws in a [neighboring] Province, establishing therein an Arbitrary government, and enlarging its Boundaries so as to render it at once an example and fit instrument for introducing the same absolute rule into these Colonies:

For taking away our Charters, abolishing our most valuable Laws, and altering fundamentally the Forms of our Governments:

For suspending our own Legislatures, and declaring themselves invested with power to legislate for us in all cases whatsoever.

He has abdicated Government here, by declaring us

out of his Protection and <u>waging War against us.</u>
He has <u>plundered our seas, ravaged our Coasts,</u>
<u>burnt our towns, and destroyed the lives of our</u>
<u>people.</u> He is at this time transporting <u>large Armies</u>
<u>of foreign Mercenaries</u> to [complete] the works of
<u>death, desolation and tyranny</u>, already begun with
circumstances of Cruelty & perfidy scarcely
paralleled in the most barbarous ages, and totally
unworthy the Head of a civilized nation.
He has <u>constrained our fellow Citizens</u> taken
Captive on the high <u>Seas to bear Arms against their</u>
<u>Country, to become the executioners of their friends</u>
<u>and Brethren,</u> or to fall themselves by their Hands.
He has <u>excited domestic insurrections</u> amongst us,
and has [endeavored] to bring on the inhabitants of
our frontiers, the <u>merciless Indian Savages,</u> whose
known rule of warfare, is an undistinguished
<u>destruction of all ages, sexes</u> and conditions.[110]

<u>EFFORTS AT RECONCILLIATION</u>. After listing the
many abuses of the King of Great Britain, the Declaration of
Independence briefly states the efforts the Colonies made to
resolve their problems with Great Britain, and the total lack of
positive response to their efforts.

<u>In every stage</u> of these Oppressions We have <u>Petitioned</u>
<u>for Redress in the most humble terms</u>: Our repeated
Petitions have been <u>answered only by repeated injury</u>.
A Prince whose character is thus marked by every act
which may define a <u>Tyrant, is unfit</u> to be the <u>ruler of a</u>
<u>free people</u>.[111]

---

[110] Ibid.
[111] <u>Ibid</u>.

FINAL SECTION. The final section of the Declaration of Independence states,

> We, therefore, the Representatives of the united
> States of America, in General Congress, Assembled,
> <u>appealing to the Supreme Judge of the
> world</u>...solemnly publish and declare, That these
> United Colonies are, and of Right ought to be <u>Free
> and Independent States</u>; that they are <u>Absolved from
> all Allegiance to the British Crown</u>, and that <u>all
> political connection</u> between them and the State of
> Great Britain, is and ought to be <u>totally dissolved</u>;
> and that as Free and Independent States, they have
> full Power to levy War, conclude Peace, contract
> Alliances, establish Commerce, and to do all other
> Acts and Things which Independent States may of
> right do. [112]

The appeal to the "Supreme Judge of the world" is an appeal to God. The last sentence of the Declaration of Independence states, "And for the support of this Declaration, with a firm reliance on the protection of divine Providence, we mutually pledge to each other our Lives, our Fortunes and our sacred Honor."[113] "Firm reliance on the protection of divine Providence" means firm reliance on God.

VOTING FOR LIFE. Voting with the Declaration of Independence requires voting Republican because it is a pro-life document. First, it affirms that all men have a god-given right to life. Second, it affirms that all men are created equal. In other words, from conception until birth God creates each person in his or her mother's womb, and makes that person equal in value to all other persons. The right to life begins at

---

[112] Ibid.
[113] Ibid.

conception, not birth. A mother's duty to care for her child begins at conception, not birth. A mother who abuses that right with drugs or alcohol endangers the health of her child. All of these views are based upon Scripture which is discussed in later chapters.

VOTING FOR LIBERTY AND PURSUIT OF HAPPINESS. Voting with the Declaration of Independence requires voting Republican because Republicans support the rights to liberty and the pursuit of happiness infinitely better than Democrats. Republicans want lower taxes for all Americans. They want all Americans to have the right and freedom to keep more of their hard-earned money, which enables the pursuit of happiness. Democrats always want the government to do more to care for Americans, which requires higher taxes and less freedom for all Americans. All of this is discussed in greater detail in later chapters.

VOTING FOR RIGHT TO BEAR ARMS. Voting with the Declaration of Independence requires voting Republican because Republicans better support the right to bear arms. The entire Declaration of Independence is an argument for the right of the people to bear arms and to use those arms to overthrow any government which violates their God-given rights to life, liberty, and the pursuit of happiness. It is not argument for them to be able to bear lower-capacity arms, but an argument to be able to bear the exact same arms that would be used against them by the government.

CONCLUSION. So what does the Declaration of Independence teach us about the Founding Fathers? First, that they had a biblical worldview. They understood that: (1) God created all things seen and unseen and all laws that govern all things seen and unseen; (2) God creates all men equal with "certain unalienable Rights that [...include] Life, Liberty and the pursuit of Happiness;" (3) "to secure these rights, Governments are instituted among Men, deriving their just powers from the consent of the governed;" (4) "whenever any...Government becomes destructive of these ends, it is the Right of the People to alter or to abolish it, and to institute new Government;" (5) this new government must be established in accordance with God's laws to protect the God-given unalienable rights of all men.[114]

So what does voting for and with the Declaration of Independence require? First and foremost, it requires voting Republican because Republicans better support all these principles that the United States was founded upon. Second, it requires voting Republican because Republicans better support the rights to life, liberty, the pursuit of happiness, and the right to bear arms.

---

[114] Ibid.

CHAPTER 6.2

VOTING FOR CONSTITUTION

INTRODUCTION. What does voting in accordance with the principles embodied in the Constitution of the United States require? Before trying to answer this question, this chapter will lay a foundation of understanding regarding: (1) law and government, (2) jurisdiction; (3) the basic duty of government, and (4) the purpose, organization, and contents of the Constitution.

LAW AND GOVERNMENT. Consider the importance of law to government. The legislative branch makes laws. The executive branch enforces the laws. The judicial branch decides cases and controversies with respect to application of the laws. In other words, the federal government makes, enforces, and decides cases or controversies regarding federal laws.

DEFINITION OF JURISDICTION. Jurisdiction is one of the most important legal principles taught in law school. Black's Law Dictionary gives an insightful definition of jurisdiction for the judicial branch of government. "A term of large and comprehensive import, and embraces every kind of judicial action...." It is the "power and authority of a court to hear and determine a judicial proceeding."[115] Black's Law Dictionary actually takes a couple pages to fully define the broad subject of jurisdiction. Readers of this book only need to know that the jurisdiction of the federal government is the "power and authority" that it has under the Constitution to

---

[115] Henry Campbell Black, Black's Law Dictionary, 5th Ed., 1979, p 766.

make, enforce, and make judgments regarding application of federal law. In other words, the United States Constitution defines the responsibility and limits of power of the United States government.

BASIC DUTY OF GOVERNMENT. Understanding of the most basic, fundamental duty of government is essential to understanding of the jurisdiction of government. "YOU CANNOT DICTATE MORALITY" read the full-page newspaper advertisement in large, bold letters. It was many years ago, but I could never forget it. Many Americans, like Biden, believe that abortion should be legal because no one has the right to "legislate morality" or to impose their morality on someone else. When asked when life began, Obama said the answer to that question was "above his pay grade." But it was not above his pay grade to decide that the unborn child must die if not wanted by the mother. He actually said that he would not want one of his daughters to be punished by being forced to give birth to an unwanted child. Were Senators Obama and Biden right or wrong? Does government have the jurisdiction (power and authority) to dictate morality?" Anyone who cannot properly answer these simple questions cannot begin to understand the role, jurisdiction, or limits of authority of government.

In his letter to the Romans, the Apostle Paul helps one more clearly understand the jurisdiction of government. Romans 13:1-7 states:

> Let every soul be in subjection to the higher
> powers: for there is no power but of God; and
> the powers that be are ordained of God.
> Therefore he that resist[s] the power,
> withstand[s] the ordinance of God: and they that

withstand shall receive to themselves judgment. For <u>rulers are not a terror to the good work, but to the evil</u>. And would thou have no fear of the power? do that which is good, and thou shalt have praise from the same: for he is a minister of God to thee for good. But if thou do that which is evil, be afraid; for he <u>bear[s] not the sword in vain: for he is a minister of God</u>, an avenger for wrath to him that doeth evil. Wherefore ye must needs be in subjection, not only because of the wrath, but also for conscience' sake. For this cause ye <u>pay tribute also; for they are ministers of God's service</u>, attending continually upon this very thing. <u>Render to all their dues: tribute to whom tribute is due; custom to whom custom; fear to whom fear; honor to whom honor</u> (Rom 13:1-7, ASV).

In other words, government officials are "ministers of God" with jurisdiction (power, authority, and responsibility) to impose morality and punish evildoers. The primary reason they have a duty to punish criminal acts is not because they harm other citizens or because punishment best serves the accused, the victim, others, or the government, but because the criminal acts are morally wrong, they demand justice, and it is their God-given duty to ensure justice in accordance with God's laws as they are revealed through Scripture.

<u>PURPOSE OF CONSTITUTION</u>. To protect the God-given unalienable rights of life, liberty, and the pursuit of happiness, and to protect citizens from the abuses of power of the King of Great Britain, the Founding Fathers drafted a Constitution which made the federal government of the United States a government of enumerated powers. Each branch of

government only had the powers granted to it by the Constitution. All other powers were reserved to the states. This book will concentrate on parts of the Constitution that state what powers are granted to the federal government, not on administrative sections.

ORGANIZATION OF CONSTITUTION. The Constitution is divided into a preamble and seven articles. The short preamble states:

> We the People of the United States, in Order to form a more perfect Union, establish Justice, insure domestic Tranquility, provide for the common [defense], promote the general Welfare, and secure the Blessings of Liberty to ourselves and our Posterity, do ordain and establish this Constitution for the United States of America.[116]

The preamble states the general purpose of the Constitution. It does not grant any powers to any branch of the federal government. If, for example, "promote the general Welfare" granted any authority, it would grant virtually unlimited authority to all branches of the federal government, which would destroy the intent of the signers to create a government of enumerated powers where each branch only had those powers granted to it by the Constitution.

ARTICLE I. The first three articles of the Constitution grant powers to the three branches of the federal government. The first, longest, most important article grants powers to a Congress. Article I is divided into ten sections. Section 1 states, "All legislative Powers herein granted shall be vested in

---

[116] "Constitution of the United States," U.S. National Archives & Records Administration, http://www.archives.gov/exhibits/charters/constitution.html.

a Congress of the United States, which shall consist of a Senate and House of Representatives." Sections 2-7 state how members of Congress are elected, serve, are paid, etc. See Appendix B for text.

Section 7 addresses raising taxes, "All Bills for raising Revenue shall originate in the House of Representatives; but the Senate may propose or concur with Amendments as on other Bills." The remainder of Section 7 reviews how bills are voted upon, passed, and become law. See Appendix B for text.

Section 8 states powers granted to Congress. Note that there is no mention of education, healthcare, or any other social programs.

> *The Congress shall have Power To lay and collect Taxes, Duties, Imposts and Excises, to pay the Debts and provide for the common Defence and general Welfare of the United States; but all Duties, Imposts and Excises shall be uniform throughout the United States;*
> *To borrow Money on the credit of the United States;*
> *To regulate Commerce with foreign Nations, and among the several States, and with the Indian Tribes;*
> To establish an uniform Rule of Naturalization, and uniform Laws on the subject of Bankruptcies throughout the United States;
> To coin Money, regulate the Value thereof, and of foreign Coin, and fix the Standard of Weights and Measures;

To provide for the <u>Punishment of counterfeiting</u> the Securities and current Coin of the United States;

To establish <u>Post Offices</u> and post Roads;

To <u>promote</u> the Progress of <u>Science and useful Arts</u>, by securing for limited Times to Authors and Inventors the <u>exclusive Right</u> to their respective <u>Writings and Discoveries</u>;

To constitute <u>Tribunals</u> inferior to the supreme Court;

To define and <u>punish Piracies</u> and Felonies committed on the high Seas, and Offences against the <u>Law of Nations</u>;

To <u>declare War</u>, grant Letters of Marque and Reprisal, and <u>make Rules</u> concerning <u>Captures</u> on Land and Water;

To raise and <u>support Armies</u>, but no Appropriation of Money to that Use shall be for a longer Term than two Years;

To provide and maintain a <u>Navy</u>;

To make <u>Rules</u> for the Government and Regulation of the <u>land and naval Forces</u>;

To provide for calling forth the <u>Militia to execute the Laws</u> of the Union, <u>suppress Insurrections and repel Invasions</u>;

To provide for <u>organizing, arming, and disciplining, the Militia</u>, and for governing such <u>Part of them</u> as may be employed in the <u>Service of the United States</u>, reserving to the States respectively, the Appointment of the Officers, and the Authority of training the Militia according to the discipline prescribed by Congress;

To exercise exclusive Legislation in all Cases whatsoever, over such <u>District</u> (not exceeding <u>ten Miles square</u>) as may, by Cession of particular States, and the Acceptance of Congress, become the <u>Seat of the Government of the United States</u>, and to exercise like Authority over all Places purchased by the Consent of the Legislature of the State in which the Same shall be, for the Erection <u>of Forts, Magazines, Arsenals, dock-Yards, and other needful Buildings</u>;--And
To <u>make all Laws</u> which shall be necessary and proper for carrying into <u>Execution the foregoing Powers</u>, and all other Powers vested by this Constitution in the Government of the United States, or in any Department or Officer thereof.

Section 9 states limitations on the powers of Congress. Section 10 states rules regarding states (treaties, duties on imports or exports, etc.). See Appendix B for text of these sections.

<u>ARTICLE II.</u> The second article of the Constitution grants powers to the President, the executive branch of the government. It is divided into four sections. Section 1 states how the President is elected, serves, is paid, etc. See Appendix B for text. Section 2 states powers granted to the President. Note that there is no mention of education, healthcare, or any other social programs.

The <u>President shall be</u> <u>Commander in Chief</u> of the Army and Navy of the United States, and of the Militia of the several States, when called into the actual Service of the United States; he may require the <u>Opinion, in writing</u>, of the principal Officer in each of the <u>executive Departments</u>, upon any Subject relating to the Duties of their respective Offices, and he shall have Power to grant <u>Reprieves and Pardons</u> for Offences against the United States, except in Cases of Impeachment.

He shall have Power, by and with the Advice and Consent of the Senate, to make <u>Treaties</u>, provided two thirds of the Senators present concur; and he shall nominate, and by and with the Advice and Consent of the Senate, shall appoint <u>Ambassadors, other public Ministers and Consuls, Judges of the supreme Court, and all other Officers</u> of the United States, whose Appointments are not herein otherwise provided for, and which shall be established by Law: but the Congress may by Law vest the Appointment of such inferior Officers, as they think proper, in the President alone, in the Courts of Law, or in the Heads of Departments.

The President shall have Power to fill up all <u>Vacancies</u> that may happen during the <u>Recess</u> of the Senate, by granting Commissions which shall expire at the End of their next Session.

Section 3 states how President will work with Congress (State of Union, etc.). Section 4 states grounds for impeachment of the President, Vice President, and all "civil Officers of the United States." See Appendix B for text.

<u>ARTICLE III</u>. The third article of the Constitution grants powers to the Supreme Court and federal courts, the judicial branch of the federal government. It is divided into

128

three sections. Section 1 states how the judges will serve, be paid, etc. Section 3 addresses treason against the United States. Only Section 2 states powers of the courts: Note that there is no mention of education, healthcare, or any other social programs.

The judicial Power shall extend to all Cases, in Law and Equity, arising under this Constitution, the Laws of the United States, and Treaties made, or which shall be made, under their Authority;--to all Cases affecting Ambassadors, other public Ministers and Consuls;--to all Cases of admiralty and maritime Jurisdiction;-- to Controversies to which the United States shall be a Party;--to Controversies between two or more States;-- between a State and Citizens of another State;--between Citizens of different States;--between Citizens of the same State claiming Lands under Grants of different States, and between a State, or the Citizens thereof, and foreign States, Citizens or Subjects.
In all Cases affecting Ambassadors, other public Ministers and Consuls, and those in which a State shall be Party, the supreme Court shall have original Jurisdiction. In all the other Cases before mentioned, the supreme Court shall have appellate Jurisdiction, both as to Law and Fact, with such Exceptions, and under such Regulations as the Congress shall make.
The Trial of all Crimes, except in Cases of Impeachment, shall be by Jury; and such Trial shall be held in the State where the said Crimes shall have been committed; but when not committed within any State, the Trial shall be at

such Place or Places as the Congress may by
Law have directed.

ARTICLE IV and ARTICLE V. The fourth article of
the Constitution only addresses issues related to the states. The
fifth article of the Constitution states the rules regarding
proposal and ratification of amendments to the Constitution.
These articles have no bearing on this book.

ARTICLE VI. The sixth article declares "this
Constitution, and the Laws of the United States which shall be
made in Pursuance thereof…the supreme Law of the Land; and
the Judges in every State shall be bound thereby…." It also
states that "Senators and Representatives…and the Members
of…State Legislatures, and all executive and judicial
Officers…of the United States and of the…States, shall be
bound by Oath or Affirmation, to support this Constitution; but
no religious Test shall ever be required as a Qualification to
any Office…"[117] Note that the requirement of "no religious
test" only applies to federal and state government officials. It
has absolutely nothing to do with qualification for immigration
or citizenship, as some Democrats have stated.

ARTICLE VII. The seventh and final article of the
Constitution only deals with details of ratification of the
Constitution by the states in 1787. It has no bearing on this
book.

CONCLUSION. So what does the Constitution say
about jurisdiction of the federal government? First,
government of the United States is a government of
enumerated powers; each branch only has those powers
granted by the Constitution. Article I grants powers to

---

[117] Ibid.

Congress (Senate and House of Representatives). Article II grants powers to the executive branch (President). Article III grants powers to the judicial branch (Supreme Court and federal courts). No part of the Constitution grants any authority regarding education, healthcare, or any other social programs. Detailed discussion of all powers granted to the federal government is beyond the scope of this book. This book concentrates on the primary problem, the exercise of powers not granted by the Constitution.

During the 2008 election, Senator Obama often quoted the words "I am my brother's keeper" to explain what motivates him to government service. However, these are not words used by Christ, but words used by Cain after killing his brother Abel (Gen. 4:9). They have nothing to do with government. Most Republicans advocate a smaller federal government, lower taxes, and greater freedom. Most Democrats want a government that does more to help the people, which means more socialism, more redistribution of wealth, higher taxes and less freedom for citizens of the larger, more powerful government, all in violation of the powers granted to the federal government by the U.S. Constitution.

Most readers probably need clarification by what is meant by "less freedom." Greater taxes to pay for more government benefits means most Americans must work longer each year just to pay their taxes. More government benefits means the government is taking more by force from most taxpayers to very ineffectively process and redistribute the funds to other taxpayers in the form of government benefits. In other words, taxpayers are forced to pay the school tuition, doctor bills and other bills of other taxpayers and much of the money they are forced to pay is spent paying for the larger government needed to ineffectively manage the government programs.

So having a government that does more to take care of its people means Americans work longer each year just to pay their taxes and have less "liberty" and less of their own money to spend however they wish in their personal "pursuit of happiness." In other words, they have less of two of three God-given inalienable rights the United States government was established to protect. Also, more money flowing through government to schools and businesses means more improper government control of and less freedom for schools and businesses. It also means more fraud, more government waste, and more improper influence of government officials.

The objective of Democrats to increase the size and cost of government to provide more benefits to citizens violates the limited powers granted to the federal government by the U.S. Constitution. The spending on social programs is unconstitutional. The federal government is a government of enumerated powers; each branch only has those powers granted to it by the Constitution. No part of the Constitution grants any power to establish social programs. This is discussed in greater detail in the chapter on the Constitution.

If elected, Democrats will continue to increase the size and cost of government, a cost which must be passed on to the taxpayers one way or another, through individual or corporate taxes. Taxpayers are the only source of income for government. There is no such thing as a free lunch. More government benefits must be paid for by taxpayers.

CHAPTER 6.3

VOTING THE BILL OF RIGHTS

INTRODUCTION. What does voting according to principles embodied in the Bill of Rights require? To answer this question, this chapter will review: (1) history/definition of Bill of Rights; (2) rights granted by the ten amendments. The First and Second Amendments are discussed in much greater detail in separate chapters. Most other amendments are not discussed in detail because they are not critical to voting Christian values in the coming election. See Appendix C for full text of the Constitution.

HISTORY/DEFINITION OF BILL OF RIGHTS. In 1789 Congress ratified the first ten amendments to the Constitution, known as the "Bill of Rights."[118] Although all of the amendments are important for protection of freedoms enjoyed by Americans, this book will only concentrate on the few cited herein.

FIRST AMENDMENT. The First Amendment grants the rights to freedom of speech, religion, press, and assembly. It states:

> Congress shall make no law respecting an establishment of religion, or prohibiting the free exercise thereof; or abridging the freedom of speech, or of the press; or the right of the people

_____

[118] "Bill of Rights," U.S. National Archives Records Administration, http://www.archives.gov/exhibits/charters/constitution.html.

peaceably to assemble, and to petition the Government for a redress of grievances.[119]

See separate chapter on Freedom of Religion, which addresses both freedom of religion and freedom of speech of Christians.

SECOND AMENDMENT. The Second Amendment grants the right to bear arms. It states: "A well regulated Militia, being necessary to the security of a free State, the right of the people to keep and bear Arms, shall not be infringed."[120] See separate chapter on Right to Bear Arms.

THIRD AMENDMENT. The Third Amendment only addresses soldiers staying in the homes of citizens with the permission of the owner. It states, " No Soldier shall, in time of peace be quartered in any house, without the consent of the Owner, nor in time of war, but in a manner to be prescribed by law."[121]

FOURTH AMENDMENT. The Fourth Amendment guards citizens from "unreasonable searches and seizures" and warrants without "probable cause." It states:

> The right of the people to be secure in their persons, houses, papers, and effects, against unreasonable searches and seizures, shall not be violated, and no Warrants shall issue, but upon probable cause, supported by Oath or affirmation, and particularly describing the

---

[119] "Bill of Rights," U.S. National Archives & Records Administration, http://www.archives.gov/exhibits/charters/constitution.html.
[120] Ibid.
[121] Ibid.

place to be searched, and the persons or things to be seized.[122]

FIFTH AMENDMENT. The Fifth Amendment grants citizens the right to freedom from prosecution unless there is "indictment by Grand Jury," "due process of law," and no double jeopardy. It also guarantees just compensation for property taken for public use.

> No person shall be held to answer for a capital, or otherwise infamous crime, unless on a presentment or indictment of a Grand Jury, except in cases arising in the land or naval forces, or in the Militia, when in actual service in time of War or public danger; nor shall any person be subject for the same offence to be twice put in jeopardy of life or limb; nor shall be compelled in any criminal case to be a witness against himself, nor be deprived of life, liberty, or property, without due process of law; nor shall private property be taken for public use, without just compensation.[123]

SIXTH AMENDMENT--RIGHT TO ATTORNEY. The Sixth Amendment grants every American accused of a crime the right to a criminal defense attorney. It states:

> In all criminal prosecutions, the accused shall enjoy the right to a speedy and public trial, by an impartial jury of the State and district wherein the crime shall have been committed, which district shall have been previously

---

[122] Ibid.
[123] Ibid.

ascertained by law, and to be informed of the
nature and cause of the accusation; to be
confronted with the witnesses against him; to
have compulsory process for obtaining
witnesses in his favor, and to have the
Assistance of Counsel for his defence.[124]

Note that there is no right to an attorney for civil cases.
There is only a right to an attorney when it is a criminal case of
the government versus the accused citizen.

SEVENTH AMENDMENT. The Seventh Amendment
grants the right to trial by jury. It states:

In Suits at common law, where the value in
controversy shall exceed twenty dollars, the
right of trial by jury shall be preserved, and
no fact tried by a jury, shall be otherwise re-
examined in any Court of the United States,
than according to the rules of the common
law.[125]

EIGHTH AMENDMENT. The Eighth Amendment
protects citizens from excessive bail. It states: "Excessive bail
shall not be required, nor excessive fines imposed, nor cruel
and unusual punishments inflicted."[126]

NINTH AMENDMENT. The Ninth Amendment
makes it clear that Americans have other rights not listed in the
Constitution or Bill of Rights. It states, "The enumeration in
the Constitution, of certain rights, shall not be construed to

---

[124] Ibid.
[125] Ibid.
[126] Ibid.

deny or disparage underlined others retained by the people."[127] In other words, the fact that the Constitution and Bill of Rights list and describe certain rights does not mean these are the only rights of citizens.

TENTH AMENDMENT. The tenth amendment states the vitally important principle that "the powers not delegated to the United States by the Constitution, nor prohibited by it to the States, are reserved to the States respectively, or to the people."[128] This vitally important amendment is additional confirmation that the federal government only has those powers that are specifically granted to it by the Constitution.

RIGHTS NOT GRANTED BY BILL OF RIGHTS. Many Americans mistakenly believe that they have many rights not granted by the Constitution or Bill of Rights. This greatly impacts politics and government. .

RIGHT TO EDUCATION. The U.S. Constitution does not grant any American the right to an education. The United States government has no constitutional authority to make any laws regarding what person or organization provides or pays for education. The federal government has no authority to grant college student loans. Many state constitutions may grant citizens the right to a public education paid for by other citizens, but there is no right to any education under the Constitution of the United States.

RIGHT TO HEALTHCARE. The U.S. Constitution does not grant any American the right to any healthcare paid for by other Americans. The United States government has no

---

[127] Ibid.
[128] Ibid.

constitutional authority to make any laws regarding what persons or organizations provide or pay for healthcare.

CONCLUSION. The Bill of Rights, the first ten amendments to the Constitution, grants all Americans the rights of freedom of religion, freedom of speech, right to bear arms, right to a criminal defense attorney, and other rights enumerated therein. The ninth amendment protects other rights of the people. The tenth amendment makes it clear that the federal government only has those powers granted to it by the Constitution, and that all other powers are reserved to the states. No part of the Constitution or Bill of Rights grants any American any right to education, healthcare, or any other social or economic benefits paid for by other Americans.

VOTING FOR RIGHTS AND FREEDOMS

SECTION REVIEW. This section shows what voting for rights and freedoms requires. Chapter 8.1 shows what voting for liberty and the pursuit of happiness requires. Chapter 8.2 shows what voting for freedom of speech and freedom of religion requires. Chapter 8.3 shows what voting for the right to bear arms requires.

CHAPTERS:
8.1 Voting for Liberty and Pursuit of Happiness
8.2 Voting for Freedom of Speech and Religion
8.3 Voting for Right to Bear Arms

VOTING FOR LIBERTY AND PURSUIT OF HAPPINESS

INTRODUCTION. Liberty and the "pursuit of happiness" are the second and third God-given inalienable rights listed in the first paragraph of the Declaration of Independence. "Life," the first inalienable right listed, is addressed in a prior chapter entitled "Abortion." An inalienable right is a God-given right that no man has a right to take away from another man. Patrick Henry's famous words, "Give me liberty, or give me death!" express the sentiment of most Americans. Americans greatly treasure the freedoms they enjoy as citizens of the United States.

DEFINITION OF LIBERTY. Today most Americans have a totally different understanding of the meaning of liberty than that given by God in scripture. Most believe that freedom is the right to do whatever is right in your own eyes, so long as doing so does not harm another person. That is totally contrary to Scripture. The words, "Every man did that which was right in his own eyes" (Judges 17:5-7; 21:24-25) describe a period of lawlessness in Israel (See Deut. 12:7-9; Prov. 12:15; 21:2). God commanded the Israelites to not do whatever was right in their own eyes, but to obey His commandments. King David said, "I will walk at liberty: for I seek thy precepts" (Ps. 119:45). In other words, true liberty is found through submission to God and obedience to His laws, not through doing whatever is right in your own eyes.

FOUNDING FATHERS AND LIBERTY. Most Americans also have a totally different understanding of the meaning of true liberty than our nation's Founding Fathers.

The Founding Fathers were never willing to exchange their freedom for government benefits. They even protested taxes on tea. In total contrast, today many Americans are willing to give up their liberty and live under much greater government taxes in exchange for government benefits. That is one of the major factors that divide Americans between Republicans and Democrats. See further discussion below, under Pursuit of Happiness.

BILL OF RIGHTS. In 1789 Congress ratified the first ten amendments to the Constitution, known as the "Bill of Rights."[129] The Bill of Rights defines key rights and freedoms of Americans. The First Amendment grants the rights to freedom of speech, religion, press, and assembly. The Second Amendment grants the right to bear arms. See chapters on Freedom of Religion, Right to Bear Arms, and Bill of Rights for discussion of rights and freedoms.

PURSUIT OF HAPPINESS. Most Americans are probably uncertain about the meaning of "pursuit of happiness." Basically, "pursuit of happiness" means the freedom to work and earn, keep, and spend money to pursue one's own happiness. Few politicians ever mention the "pursuit of happiness", but it plays a key role in every national election. Most Republicans want smaller government and lower taxes. They want all Americans to have the right and freedom to keep more of their hard-earned money, which enables the pursuit of happiness.

Democrats always want a larger government which does more to take care of its people and they are willing to have others pay higher taxes to fund it. If asked individually,

---

[129] "Bill of Rights," U.S. National Archives & Records Administration, http://www.archives.gov/exhibits/charters/constitution.html.

most Democrats are probably not personally willing to pay higher taxes, and most Democratic politicians would never tell their supporters that they have to personally pay higher taxes to receive more government benefits. Democrats and the Democratic Platform always claim that they only want to raise taxes on the "wealthy few" who are not paying their "fair share", but that is a lie. Totally contrary to what Democrats and the Democratic Platform claim, the middle class does not pay its fair share of taxes and the wealthy pay far more than their fair share. All of this is discussed in greater detail in chapter on Truth on Taxes.

DECLARATION OF INDEPENDENCE. Voting with the Declaration of Independence requires voting Republican because Republicans support the right to liberty infinitely better than Democrats. First, more Republicans support God's definition of liberty, which requires obedience to God's commandments, not doing whatever is right in your own eyes. Second, Republicans want smaller government and lower taxes, which means greater liberty to exercise the pursuit of happiness. Third, more Republicans more strongly support the right to bear arms, so important to the Founding Fathers not just for hunting or personal protection, but for the establishment and defense of the United States.

CONSTITUTION. The Constitution of the United States of America was carefully and deliberately designed to strictly limit the power and authority of the federal government, and to reserve all other powers to the people and the states. In other words, the Constitution was designed to greatly limit the powers of the federal government to maximize the freedom of the people. However, countless years of voting to increase the size and power of the federal government have greatly increased federal taxes and greatly reduced the power of the people to engage in the pursuit of happiness. In other words, continually voting to increase the role of the federal government has greatly reduced the ability of Americans to keep and spend the money that they have earned.

CHAPTER 7.2

VOTING FOR FREEDOM OF SPEECH AND FREEDOM OF RELIGION

INTRODUCTION. Freedom of speech and freedom of religion are two of the most important rights of every American. They are also the most infringed upon and threatened rights of Christians. The First Amendment to the Constitution grants the rights freedom of speech and freedom of religion. It states:

> Congress shall make no law resecting an establishment of religion, or prohibiting the free exercise thereof; or abridging the freedom of speech, or of the press; or the right of the people peaceably to assemble, and to petition the Government for a redress of grievances.[130]

DEMOCRATS AGAINST CHRISTIANS. Democrats have repeatedly tried to enact laws to silence Christians, to eliminate their competition during national elections. No group of Americans has more restrictions on its freedom of speech and freedom of religion than Christians. The U.S. Supreme Court actually approved the use of laws against anti-abortion protestors laws that were designed to be used against organized crime. During 2008, Democrats tried to enact legislation to silence Christian and conservative talk shows. The Obama Administration's attempt to force Catholic and other religious institutions to provide contraceptives, abortions, abortive drugs, and other medical products or procedures that violated

---

[130] "Bill of Rights," U.S. National Archives & Records Administration, http://www.archives.gov/exhibits/charters/constitution.html.

their religious or moral convictions was one of the most egregious violations of the First Amendment to the U.S. Constitution by a President.[131]

A law nicknamed the LBJ law because President Lyndon Baines Johnson signed it to silence his critics, threatens the tax-exempt status of any church or religious organization that endorses any candidate. It is is a totally unconstitutional violation of the First Amendment. It is a tool effectively used by Democrats to silence Christians. Every religious leader has a duty to provide moral guidance to his congregation regarding all areas of life, to include politics. The Founding Fathers would be absolutely shocked to learn that pastors have been silenced in the name of "separation of church and state." Today most judges fail to realize that these laws are clear violations of freedom of speech and freedom of religion.

The author of this book had the honor of asking U.S. Supreme Court Justice Anthony Scalia one question during his visit to Regent University. He asked why the Supreme Court permitted the voice of moral leaders to be silenced. Justice Scalia asked if he would give the same rights to an ACLU attorney. When he said that he would be inclined to do so, Scalia said that he did not have a logical problem, but that the hands of the Supreme Court were tied by Congress, meaning by the LBJ law. Justice Scalia should be respected for his response. Many liberal judges show little respect for laws enacted by Congress or state legislatures. However, the author respectfully disagrees. The Supreme Court is one of the three branches of the federal government with responsibility to serve as part of the checks and balances established by the Founding

---

[131] "Where Do the Candidates Stand on Life: Mitt Romney, Barack Obama," National Right to Life Committee, http://www.nrlc.org.

Fathers. It has a duty to correct Congress when they enact a law that is so clearly a violation of the U.S. Constitution's protections of freedom of religion and freedom of speech. See Bill of Rights, Appendix C.

SEPARATION OF CHURCH AND STATE. Most Americans believe in separation of church and state, but differ sharply in what they believe it means. Many believe that the words "separation of church and state" are in the U.S. Constitution. They are not. They were first used by Thomas Jefferson to refer to the need to keep the church free from interference by government and to not have a state church improperly ruled by the government as in England. Over one hundred years later, they were used by the Supreme Court to define the limits of authority of church and state. Today many Americans believe in separation of church and state in a way that would be anathema to the Founding Fathers. Democrats have reversed the meaning of Jefferson's words, using them to justify action against the church and to silence Christian leaders, a violation of their rights to freedom of religion and freedom of speech. See Bill of Rights, Appendix C.

BELIEF IN GOD. Today many Americans believe that separation of church and state means that teachers and elected officials cannot rightfully be expected to believe in God or creation because these are matters of personal faith that do not belong in public schools, government, or the workplace. This is totally contrary to Scripture, common sense, and the beliefs of the Founding Fathers.

Belief in God and creation does not require faith. It only requires a modicum of common sense. "We hold these truths to be self-evident, that all men are created equal, that they are endowed by their Creator with certain unalienable

Rights...." (Declaration of Independence, Appendix A.) The United States was founded upon belief in God and creation. The Founding Fathers understood that belief in God, creation, and God's laws were common sense, self-evident truths. The most amazing common sense, self-evident truth embraced by the founding fathers was that God continues to create all men within their mothers, and to endow them with certain God-given unalienable rights which no man or government can rightfully take from another man. The Founding Fathers believed that it was the violation of these rights that justified the Declaration of Independence, Revolutionary War, and establishment of the United States of America.

Anyone who does not believe in God and creation is a fool. No fool should be trusted with any teaching or leadership position. King David said, "The fool has said in his heart, 'There is no God.'" (Psalm 14:1-3; 53:1-3). In other words, only a fool refuses to acknowledge the existence of God. Scripture teaches through King Solomon and other authors of Proverbs, that the fear of God is the beginning of wisdom.

Belief in God does not constitute endorsement of any religion. Many religions believe in God, and many individuals who are not part of any known religion believe in God. Belief in Christ is totally different. Neither Scripture nor the Founding Fathers stated that knowledge of Christ is a common sense, self-evident truth. God has not revealed Christ through creation. It takes acceptance of a gift of faith from God to believe in Christ because the cross is foolishness to man but the wisdom and power of God (1 Cor. 1:18-25). Belief in Christ as the Son of God is a tenant of one religion—Christianity.

ACKNOWLEDGMENT OF GOD. Do Christian and non-Christian teachers, professors, employers, judges, and government leaders have a right to impose their personal belief in God and creation upon their students, employees, courts, and citizens? Yes! All Americans have a duty to acknowledge God as the Creator of all things seen and unseen and of the laws that govern all things seen and unseen.

Why do all Americans, especially those in teaching or leadership positions, have a duty to acknowledge God? First, it is not because the Founding Fathers or Declaration of Independence acknowledged God. No one has any obligation to acknowledge anything just because the Founding Fathers acknowledged it. Second, it is not because Scripture acknowledges God. Scripture acknowledges Christ as Lord and Savior, but non-Christians cannot be required to acknowledge Christ as Savior. However, Scripture does explain why the Founding Fathers and the Declaration of Independence properly acknowledged God.

In his letter to the Romans, the Apostle Paul wrote,

For the wrath of God is revealed from heaven against all ungodliness and unrighteousness of men, who hold the truth in unrighteousness; Because that which may be known of God is manifest in them; for God hath shewed it unto them. For the invisible things of him from the creation of the world are clearly seen, being understood by the things that are made, even his eternal power and Godhead; so that they are without excuse: Because that, when they knew God, they glorified him not as God, neither were thankful; but became vain in their

148

imaginations, and their foolish heart was darkened. Professing themselves to be wise, they became fools…" (Romans 1:18-22, KJV).

First, many Americans believe that they have complete freedom to choose whether or not to believe in God. They do not. No man has any excuse for failure to believe in God because God has revealed the "invisible things" about Himself, including His "eternal power and Godhead," to all men so "they are without excuse." These "invisible things" about God are "clearly seen, being understood by the things that are made." In other words, God reveals Himself to man through creation. Also, "that which may be known of God is manifest in them" (in all men). God personally reveals Himself to all men.

Second, many Americans live as though they do not presently answer to God for their actions. They are wrong. The "wrath of God **is** revealed" (present tense) against "all ungodliness and unrighteousness of men." In other words, Americans are suffering the wrath of God today.

Third, Americans fail to understand why they suffer God's wrath. They suffer because they "glorified him not as God, neither were thankful." In other words, they suffer because they failed to properly acknowledge God and be thankful for His many blessings.

Fourth, Americans fail to understand how they suffer the wrath of God. "Because… they glorified him not as God, neither were thankful" they "became vain in their imaginations, and their foolish heart was darkened. Professing themselves to be wise, they became fools…" Those words describe many Americans today. They think they are wise, but they are fools. They cannot see the light of the truth because their hearts are darkened. They have become vain and foolish in their thinking.

Vain and foolish thinking are not the only ways Americans suffer God's judgment. The "wrath of God is revealed from heaven against all ungodliness and unrighteousness of men." In other words, Americans suffer the wrath of God for "all ungodliness and unrighteousness."

Consider the ignorance and foolishness of teachers and professors who believe that they can properly teach their students without teaching the self-evident, common sense truths embodied in the Declaration of Independence i.e. that God is the Creator of all things seen and unseen, to include all students, and the Creator of all laws that govern all things seen and unseen, to include all laws of mathematics and science, and laws that govern men and governments.

God has ordained that man must live by faith. Every man has a faith or religion that is his reason for living. The most important thing taught in schools is not reading, writing, arithmetic, or other academic subjects. It is faith. Today students are taught to not acknowledge or have faith in God and not to respect, fear, love or serve God or lead God-centered lives. They are taught that life is a meaningless product of evolutionary chance and that they should have faith in themselves, lead self-centered lives, and do whatever is right in their own eyes, without reference to God or His unchanging moral laws, laws rooted in His unchanging character.

Consider the ignorance of judges who have studied law for years, but refuse to acknowledge the Supreme Lawgiver, the God who created the laws that govern all things seen and unseen. They are fools who cannot be trusted to render wise judgments. Examples are liberal justices on the Supreme Court who rule totally contrary to God's laws.

Consider foolishness of government leaders who fail to properly acknowledge God. They cannot be trusted to enact, enforce, or properly adjudicate laws in accordance with God's laws. Examples include members of Congress who vote totally contrary to God's laws.

The greatest fools are those who have studied science or law but cannot see the Creator or Supreme Lawgiver; they cannot see the forest because there are so many trees. Many government leaders do great harm to our beloved nation by failing to acknowledge God, ask for His much needed guidance and blessings, and making, enforcing, and judging laws in accordance with God's laws. Many teachers and professors do great injury to and handicap their students by teaching them that they can determine truth and right and wrong without God or His laws. All Americans, especially teachers and government leaders, have a duty to properly acknowledge God, pray for His guidance and blessings, and live and vote in accordance with His laws.[132]

CONCLUSION. The Founding Fathers of the United States had a godly, biblical understanding of the jurisdiction of church and state clearly reflected in the Declaration of Independence, which began with what they clearly understood to be the only proper justification for declaration of

---

[132] George Washington would not allow his troops to curse, for fear of losing God's blessings. All Americans should be familiar with the beautiful painting of General Washington during the Revolutionary War, kneeling in the snow, praying for God's guidance and blessing. Americans need godly Christian leaders like George Washington in government.

independence from Great Britain. That justification was based upon understanding that: (1) God created all things seen and unseen and all the laws that govern all things seen and unseen; (2) God continues to create all men equal, with certain God-given unalienable rights; and (3) only repeated extreme violation of these rights justified declaration of independence and the establishment of a new government.

Today most Americans, to include most lawyers and judges, have a totally wrong understanding of the jurisdiction of church and state and the simple self-evident common sense truths that this nation was founded upon. They exclude God, creation, and God's laws from politics, government, schools, and the workplace. They completely fail to recognize that all Americans have an absolute duty to properly acknowledge God in politics, government, schools, and the workplace in the same way that our nation's Founding Fathers acknowledged Him. They also completely fail to understand that failure to properly acknowledge, respect and fear God reduces one to vain thinking and foolishness because darkened hearts cannot see the light of truth. They fail to recognize this because they have already suffered the judgment of God due to their failure to properly acknowledge Him in all areas.

If Clinton is elected and Democrats have a majority in the House and Senate, Congress will enact laws to further restrict the freedom of speech and freedom of religion of Christians. If Clinton is elected, she will appoint liberal federal judges and/or Supreme Court Justices who do not understand or respect the limits of authority imposed on government by the Constitution and legislate from the bench to further restrict the freedom of speech and freedom of religion of Christians and other Americans.

VOTING FOR THE RIGHT TO BEAR ARMS

INTRODUCTION. Americans are sharply divided on gun control and the right to bear arms. More specifically, virtually all Americans agree that there is a constitutional right to bear arms, but they sharply disagree on what type of weapons are justified by the Constitution. Some Democrats have made remarks like, "You don't need an assault weapon to hunt deer." Many Democrats want to ban ownership of all "assault weapons." These Democrats need to read and comply with the words and message of the Declaration of Independence and the Second Amendment to the Constitution.

SECOND AMENDMENT. The Second Amendment to the Constitution grants the right to bear arms. It states: "A well regulated Militia, being necessary to the security of a free State, the right of the people to keep and bear Arms, shall not be infringed."[133] Note that the absolute "right of the people to keep and bear Arms" which "shall not be infringed" is linked to the need for a "well regulated Militia" for defense of the government. The primary need for the arms, as stated in the Second Amendment, is not for hunting or self-defense, but for defense of the government. Therefore the type of weapons justified by the Second Amendment is not for hunting or self-defense, but for defense of the government.

DECLARATION OF INDEPENDENCE. The entire Declaration of Independence is an argument for the right of the people to bear arms and to use those arms to overthrow any government which violates their God-given rights to life,

---

[133] Ibid.

liberty, and the pursuit of happiness. It is not argument for them to be able to bear lower-capacity arms, but an argument to be able to bear the exact same arms that would be used against them by the government. Voting with the Declaration of Independence requires voting Republican because Republicans better support the right to bear arms.

ASSAULT WEAPONS. Neither Republicans nor Democrats would allow ownership of fully automatic weapons like those used by our armed forces. Therefore the primary issue is whether individuals should be allowed to own "assault weapons." The AR-15, a semi-automatic rifle which looks like the fully-automatic M-16 rifle, is the most popular weapon in the United States. There will therefore never be a ban on assault weapons unless Democrats win control of both the Presidency and Congress.

As an Army officer, I fired many different types of weapons from pistols, rifles, machine guns, and grenade launchers to 105mm artillery and 20mm anti-aircraft cannon (Gatling gun), and qualified on the .45 caliber pistol, 9mm pistol, and M-16 rifle many times. The AR-15 may look like the M-16 rifle, but it is only a semi-automatic rifle. It functions exactly the same as all other semi-automatic hunting rifles. You must pull the trigger for each shot. It is actually less powerful than many hunting rifles. The bullets are very small diameter (.223 caliber; 5.56 mm), and the cartridges have less powder than most other rifle cartridges. It would be ridiculous to ban "assault weapons" just because they look like military weapons, and it would be impossible to ban all semi-automatic rifles. I would only use a semi-automatic hunting rifle, because a bolt-action, lever-action, or pump-action weapon force you to lose your sight picture to chamber each round. Magazine capacity is another issue, beyond the scope of this book because it is not an issue in this election.

BACKGROUND CHECKS. Republicans and Democrats should be able to agree upon reasonable background checks. All Americans understand the need to pass a driving test before being given a driving license. All Americans should also understand the need to pass a background test before buying a weapon. Americans with mental illness should not be able to buy weapons. Americans who are on a do-not-fly terror watch-list should not be able to buy weapons. Americans who have been convicted of certain violent crimes should not be permitted to buy weapons. Republicans and Democrats should ignore demands of the NRA and come to reasonable agreement regarding background checks.

CONCLUSION. The Declaration of Independence and the Second Amendment both provide justification for the right to bear arms not for hunting or self-defense, but for defense of good government or overthrow of an abusive government that denies the God-given inalienable rights of life, liberty, and the pursuit of happiness. Thus both the Declaration of Independence and the Second Amendment provide justification for the ownership of military style weapons needed for defense or overthrow of a government. Nevertheless, Republicans and Democrats should agree to reasonable background checks and reasonable restrictions on who should be denied the right to bear arms.

CHAPTER 8.0

VOTING FOR TRUTH AND CHARACTER

SECTION REVIEW. This section addresses issues related to truth and character. Chapter 5.1 presents an alphabetical list of lies of politicians. Chapter 5.2 discusses the character of the presidential candidates. Chapter 5.3 presents facts that prove totally false the claims of Democrats and the Democratic Platform that the "wealthy few" do not pay their fair share of taxes and that the middle class pays more than its fair share. Chapter 5.4 shows that the Democratic Platform was established upon a foundation of lies, and that if you remove those lies, the Democratic Platform collapses.

CHAPTERS:
8.1 False Claims of Politicians
8.2 Voting for Character in President
8.3 Truth about Taxes
8.4 Democratic Platform: Foundation of Lies

CHAPTER 8.1

FALSE CLAIMS OF POLITICIANS

INTRODUCTION. This critically important chapter exposes many false claims made by politicians to win votes. It presents a brief, alphabetical list of these claims, and references other chapters for additional facts and more detailed discussion.

ABORTION. Most Democrats and a few Republicans claim to be pro-choice but totally reject the right to choose of pro-life Americans. They actually want to force Americans who believe that abortion is murder to pay for abortions through taxpayer funding of abortions. That is the height of hypocrisy. President Obama is the perfect example. He actually overrode the votes of governors, state legislators, and pro-life Americans by funding Planned Parenthood, the nation's largest provider of abortions, in states where the governor and state legislators cut funding. Pro-choice Americans also claim that a child is not a child with a right to life until after birth. That is totally contrary to the position of God revealed through scripture. See chapter on Scripture on Abortion for verses and detailed discussion.

CONSTITUTION. Democrats falsely claim or imply that they support the Constitution better than Republicans. The entire purpose of the Constitution is to define the jurisdiction and limits of power of each branch of the federal government. Democrats totally reject the limits of power that the Constitution places on the federal government. Most Democrats and some Republicans believe that the Constitution grants rights to education and healthcare and other social or economic benefits. It does not. All Supreme Court rulings which grant these powers are unconstitutional. See chapter on Constitution, Supreme Court, Education, and Healthcare for detailed discussion.

DECLARATION OF INDEPENDENCE. Democrats believe that they better support the ideals embodied in the Declaration of Independence. The opposite is true. Republicans better support all the principles that the United States was founded upon, and the rights to life, liberty, and the pursuit of happiness, and the right to bear arms. See chapter on Declaration of Independence for detailed discussion.

DEMOCRATIC PLATFORM. The Democratic Platform is founded upon lies. If you remove those lies, the Democratic Platform collapses. First, it is founded upon the lies that the "rich" or "wealthy few" do not pay their fair share of federal taxes, and the poor and middle class pay more than their fair share. Those are lies proven false by facts cited in the chapters on Truth on Taxes and the Democratic Platform.

EDUCATION. Democrats tell some of their biggest lies regarding education. Now Hillary Clinton is offering free college education to all families who earn less than $125,000/year (83% of all families) and debt free education to all others. Clinton claims that to pay for these benefits she will only raise taxes on the rich and corporations. The rich are already paying virtually all federal taxes. The top 1% is already paying about 27% of all federal income taxes. US corporations are already paying some of the highest corporate taxes in the world. College debt exceeds credit card debt in the United States. Obama has doubled the national debt without giving free college. There is no way that Democrats can pay for all the educational benefits that they are promising, but the false promises win millions of votes.

GOVERNMENT—ROLE OF. Most Democrats and some Republicans state, imply, or simply believe that God and the Constitution support having a government that cares for its people through social and economic programs like education and healthcare. That is an absolute lie embraced by so many Americans. Neither scripture nor the Constitution support having a government that cares for its people through social or economic programs. See chapters on Constitution and Biblical Role of Government.

HEALTHCARE. Democrats tell some of their greatest lies regarding healthcare. They promise healthcare to all Americans by only raising taxes on the rich. The rich are already paying virtually all federal income taxes. The top 1% is already paying about 27% of all federal income taxes.

HOMOPHOBIC/HOMOSEXUALITY. Americans who oppose the homosexual lifestyle are called homophobic. That is not true. Phobic means fear. Americans who oppose the homosexual lifestyle are not afraid of homosexuals. They, like God, believe that homosexuality is a perversion of God's design for man and woman. See chapter on Homosexuality and Same-Sex Marriage.

RIGHT TO BEAR ARMS. Most Democrats and some Republicans falsely claim that Constitutional right to bear arms does not include assault weapons. Some even make the foolish and irrelevant comment that "You don't need an assault weapon to hunt deer." The Constitution does not say anything about hunting. It grants the right to bear arms suitable for a "Militia" for defense of government. The entire Declaration of

Independence is justification for weapons needed to overthrow a government which fails to protect the rights to life, liberty, and the pursuit of happiness.

SAME-SEX MARRIAGE. Most Democrats and some Republicans support same-sex marriage. They say that it is a constitutional right. It is not. I was not for over 200 years and what is constitutional has not suddenly changed with the culture. Some actually believe that it is God's will. It is not. It is an extreme perversion of God's design for man, woman, and marriage. See chapter on Homosexuality and Same-Sex Marriage.

SEPARATION OF CHURCH AND STATE. Most Democrats and many Republicans believe that separation of church and state means that church leaders should not be able to endorse or recommend political candidates without their church losing its tax exempt status. That is a lie; it is a violation of their constitutional First Amendment rights to freedom to speech and freedom of religion. Politics is faith in action and religious leaders have a duty to provide voting guidance to their people. See chapter on and Freedom of Speech and Freedom of Religion.

Most Democrats and some Republicans also believe that separation of church and state means that teaching belief in God and creation should be banned from public schools. The Declaration of Independence shows that the United States was founded upon belief in God and creation, and belief that God created the laws that govern men and nations. It is therefore illogical and unethical to claim that separation of church and state does not permit teaching God and creation in public schools. See chapter on Declaration of Independence.

SUPREME COURT. Democrats claim that they are better able to select justices for the Supreme Court. They are not. Democrats never nominate, appoint, or confirm Supreme Court justices who will uphold the Constitution. To do so would be contrary to their core values. They only nominate, appoint, and confirm justices who will ignore the limits of power which the Constitution places on each branch of the federal government and grant totally unconstitutional education and healthcare benefits to Americans. Also, when Democrats have a majority in the Senate, they block pro-life Christians from the Supreme Court. See chapters on Supreme Court and Constitution.

TAXES. Democrats and the Democratic Platform claim that the "rich" or "wealthy few" do not pay their fair share of federal taxes, and that the poor and middle class pay more than their fair share. Those lies are proven false by facts cited in the chapters on Truth on Taxes and the Democratic Platform.

WOMEN'S WAGES. During the 2016 Democratic Convention, one of the speakers said that women earn only 79 cents for every dollar men earn. That conveys a totally false impression of extreme sexual discrimination. Unmarried women earn 94 to 95 cents for every dollar men earn. And some unmarried women also get pregnant, have children, and choose to leave the work force.

CONCLUSION. Politics is faith in action. It is a battle between truth and lies, right and wrong. A house divided against itself cannot stand. God is never on both sides of any war. Neither is he on both sides of the battle between Republicans and Democrats. Satan is the father of lies. Those who serve him use lies to advance their cause. This chapter presents an amazing list of lies used by Democrats to win votes. The Democratic Platform is founded upon lies. If you remove the lies, the Democratic Platform collapses. See all chapters listed within this chapter for additional supporting facts and more detailed discussion.

CHAPTER 8.2

VOTING FOR CHARACTER
IN PRESIDENT

INTRODUCTION. Jesus said, "I am the way, the truth, and the life" (John 14:6, NKJV). Truth and truthfulness are very important to God. They are an essential part of His character, His being, a vital part of who He is. This chapter discusses the truthfulness of the presidential candidates.

AMERICAN HISTORY. First, imagine yourself in an American History class in any elementary school in the 1950's. The textbooks tell stories that teach children the importance of character. One story is about President Washington as a young boy. "I cannot tell a lie," he told his father, when asked if he had chopped down the cherry tree. Another story and picture are about General Washington, kneeling in the snow at Valley Forge, praying for God's blessing and protection for his soldiers. Other stories are about President Lincoln, known as "Honest Abe," walking miles as a young boy to return a few pennies. The message of all the stories is very clear: character is important for everyone, especially for public officials, who should set a good example for all Americans.

Now, fast forward to the 1990's. Democratic members of Congress have gathered at the White House to show their support for President Bill Clinton, who has lied under oath about having sexual relations with an intern in the Oval Office. He is the only president to be disbarred as an attorney for having lied under oath. President Clinton, his wife Hillary, and all the Democrats supporting them claim that all the marital infidelity of the President is a private matter which has no bearing on his ability to discharge his duties as President. They send a completely different message to all Americans: character is not important, and there is no need for public officials to set an example of good moral character.

CLINTON CASH (book and free online video). **Americans who want to understand the depth of political corruption of the Clintons should take time to google and watch the free online video "Clinton Cash" or read the book "Clinton Cash: The Untold Story of How and Why Foreign Governments and Businesses Helped Make Bill and Hillary Rich**" by Peter Schweizer.[134] It is amazing how many millions of dollars were given to the Clinton Foundation or paid to the Clintons for speeches in exchange for political favors which greatly profited millionaires, billionaires, and enemies of the United States at the expense of Americans, people of other nations, and the environment.

All of these "pay to play" deals made the Clintons very wealthy. One deal negotiated by Hillary gave Russia 20% of United States uranium production, a very rare element needed by the United States for its own nuclear power plants and nuclear weapons. A deal with India gave American nuclear technology to India. One deal permitted the sale of Swedish technology to Iran. One donor to the Clinton Foundation got approval to deforest a rain forest in Bogota and sell the wood to China. In another Hillary reversed her position on the Keystone Excel Pipeline, turning against environmentalists, for money. Deals in Haiti enriched Clinton donors while leaving poor earthquake victims without desperately needed support.

---

[134] Peter Schweizer. Clinton Cash: The Untold Story of How and Why Foreign Governments and Businesses Helped Make Bill and Hillary Rich, New York: Harper Publishers, 2015.

Another deal enriched a corrupt leader in Nigeria without helping the poor people that needed support. [135]

ASSOCIATED PRESS REPORT: In August, 2016, the Associated Press reported that "85 of the 154 people from non-government-related interests who met with or who had scheduled phone calls with Clinton either donated to her family's charitable organization or had committed funds."[136] Clinton attacked the press, claiming that the report, which covered most of the first half of her tenure as Secretary of State, was an incomplete flawed study i.e. not proof of political corruption. That is like the Captain of the Titanic claiming that the big iceberg above water is not proof of any iceberg below water. Most of the iceberg is below water.

LAUREATE UNIVERSITY. **While Hillary Clinton was promising to "crackdown" on the "abusive practices" of "for-profit universities"** and criticizing Trump about Trump University, **Bill Clinton was paid 17.6 million dollars** over a five year period simply **for being the "honorary chancellor" of a large for-profit university** called Laureate University. Also during this same period, the founder of Laureate University gave 5 million dollars to the Clinton Foundation. See article, "Bill Clinton Got $17.6M from Big For-Profit University while Hillary Clinton Vowed 'Crackdown' on their 'Abusive Practices'" by Adam Edelman.[137]

---

[135] Ibid.

[136] Nick Gass, "Clinton mounts full-court press against media," www.politico.com/story/2016/08/clinton-campaign-blasts-massive," downloaded August 24, 2016.

[137] Adam Edelman, "Bill Clinton Got $17.6M from Big For-Profit University while Hillary Clinton Vowed 'Crackdown' on their 'Abusive Practices,'" New York Daily News, August 24, 2016.

CRISIS IN CHARACTER (book). Americans who want better understanding of the character of the Clintons may **read "Crisis in Character," a book written by former Secret Service Agent Gary J. Byrne,**[138] who worked with the Clintons in the White House. He was so shocked by the moral depravity of the Clintons that he wrote a book to document what he observed.

HILLARY'S AMERICA (book and movie). Americans who want better understanding of how Hillary Clinton developed into someone whose values are totally contrary to the principles that the United States was founded upon can **read the book or see the movie "Hillary's America: The Secret History of the Democratic Party"** by Dinesh D'Souza.[139]

AMERICA: IMAGINE A WORLD WITHOUT HER (book or movie). Americans who want to more fully understand the flawed ideology and moral bankruptcy of Democrats and other progressives, to include Obama and the Clintons, may read the book America: Imagine a World Without Her by Dinsh D'Souza.[140] They can also watch the movie: America: Imagine the World Without Her by America Film LLC, authored by Dinsh D'Souza, John Sullivan, Bruce Schooley.[141]

---

[138]Gary J. Byrne, Crisis in Character, New York: Center Street Publishers, 2016.

[139] Dinesh D'Souza, Hillary's America: The Secret History of the Democratic Party, Regenery Publishing, 2016.

[140] Dinsh D'Souza, America: Imagine a World Without Her, Regenery Publishing, 2014.

[141] Dinsh D'Souza, John Sullivan, Bruce Schooley, America: Imagine the World Without Her, America Film LLC, 2014.

HILLARY CLINTON. Now fast-forward to 2015 and 2016. First, why, under President Obama and Secretary Clinton, were two compounds in Benghazi, Algeria, one with a U.S. ambassador, under attack for 13 hours without receiving any significant military support? See the move "13 Hours" for the story of the battles. And why did Clinton lie to Americans about the attack? Why did she tell her daughter and others that it was a terrorist attack, but tell the American people and survivors of the victims that it was not? Why could she not be truthful?

Second, Hillary Clinton was dishonest regarding her emails as Secretary of State. Why did she delete over 31,380 emails? What was she trying to hide from Americans? Was she trying to hide evidence of deals with foreign governments and businesses that made the Clinton's rich? Was she trying to hide evidence of classified emails on her private server? There is no way to know, because they are "gone, but deleting that many emails is an attempt to hide a lot of information from Americans.[142]

Third, Hillary Clinton was the only Secretary of State in the history of the United States to exclusively use a private email address and private server to send some of the highest level communications of the United States government, and the only one to not use an @state.gov email address (from 2009 to 2013). It was a decision that reflects foolishness, ignorance, and careless disregard for the security of the United States. If a private in the Army did that, he would probably be court-martialed and given a dishonorable discharge, even if

---

[142] "Why Did Hillary Clinton Need a Private Server? The Answer Makes Bernie Sanders President;" TheHuffingtonPost.com, Inc., downloaded March 7, 2016.

none of the communications were classified. Lt. General Michael Flynn said, "If it were me, I would have been out the door and probably in jail." Ibid. However, some of the emails were actually classified. Hillary Clinton actually sent top-level secret classified communications of the United States over a private server.

Russia, China, Iran, South Korea, and Germany tried to hack into Clinton's emails. Former Secretary of Defense Robert Gates believes that Russia, China, or Iran may have succeeded. Edward Snowden says it's "ridiculous" to believe Clinton's emails were safe. Computer World claims that her email system was not secure for 2 months. Dan Metcalfe said, "Hillary's Email Defense Is Laughable...I should know--I ran FOIA for the U.S. government." Ibid.

Fourth, Hillary Clinton likes to convey the false impression that she is so much more civil, kinder, "nicer" than Donald Trump. Viewing videos of her 2008 attacks on President Bush and Senator Obama reveal her real character. She was extremely critical, nasty, and mean-spirited. Also, she deliberately used the parents of a fallen soldier to viciously attack Trump, then she joined the media in attacking him for every response to the verbal assault. Americans prefer fairness in competition. Most would not want to see a boxing match where one boxer has his hands tied behind his back. But the Clintons and Democrats will lie and cheat in every way possible to win.

CONCLUSION. No presidential candidate in the history of the United States and their spouse have demonstrated as many problems with character, truthfulness, and political corruption as Hillary Clinton and her husband Bill Clinton. As Secretary of State, Hillary negotiated deals with wealthy men and nations which made the Clintons very wealthy in exchange for political favors which actually hurt the United States and its allies. Also, at the same time that she was promising to "crackdown" on the "abusive practices" of "for-profit universities," Bill Clinton was paid 17.6 million dollars for being the "honorary chancellor" for a very large for-profit university and the founder donated 5 million dollars to the Clinton Fund.

A former secret service agent who worked with the Clintons in the White House was so shocked by their moral depravity that he wrote a book entitled "Crisis in Character." Hillary repeatedly lied to Americans regarding Benghazi, her emails as Secretary of State, and Trump. She promised voters far more than she can possibly deliver i.e. healthcare, tuition-free and debt-free college, etc. Trump may have a tendency to exaggerate, but he does not have the major problems with truthfulness, character, or political corruption that the Clintons have so clearly demonstrated. Voters who care about truthfulness and character in their president should vote for Trump.

CHAPTER 8.3

TRUTH ON TAXES

INTRODUCTION. "Fairness" in taxation is one of the primary themes of Democrats. It sounds so American, so right for a nation "with liberty and justice for all." All they ask in the name of fairness is that rich Americans pay their "fair" share of taxes. So why in the world would Republicans object? Who is right and why?

Democrats and the Democratic Platform claim that "rich" or "the wealthy few" are not paying their fair share of taxes and should be taxed more to support the overtaxed "middle class." These statements are totally false. First, about half of Americans, mostly middle and lower class, do not pay any federal taxes. Second, the rich pay much higher taxes than the poor or middle class.

FEDERAL INCOME TAX RATES. Current official U.S. federal income tax rates range from 10% for the lowest income group to 39.6% for the highest income group (see "2015 Tax Rate Schedules" on page 102 of 2015 Form 1040 Instructions booklet). However, actual tax rates are very different for all groups, due to countless tax deductions and credits that, contrary to the totally false impression given by Democrats, benefit the poor and middle classes much more than the wealthy. The end result is that about 49% of Americans, mostly lower and middle income, pay no federal income tax.

To view tax rates, look at the 2015 Tax Rate Schedules in the Instructions for Form 1040, page 102. Singles earning up to $9,225 pay 10% federal income tax. Those earning $9,225 to $37,450 pay $9,225 plus 15% of the amount over $9225. Those earning $37,450 to $90,750 pay $5,156 plus $25% of the amount over $37,450. Those earning $90,750 to $189,300 pay $18,482 plus 28% of the amount over $90,750. Those earning $189,300 to $411,500 pay $46,075 plus 33% of the amount over $189,300. Those earning $411,500 to $413,200 pay $119,401 plus 35% of the amount over $411,500. Those earning over $413,200 pay $119.996 plus 39.6% of the amount over $413,200. In other words, the rich pay much higher tax rates than the poor or middle class.

However, tax rates are only half of the story; deductions are the other half. The poor and middle class get many tax deductions that are phased out for the rich. The end result is that about half of Americans, mostly middle and lower class, do not pay any federal income taxes. In other words, they pay nothing to support the American soldiers who put their lives on the line for them. They pay nothing for the federal roads the travel on. They pay nothing for many benefits that they get from the federal government. Those who receive Social Security and Medicare benefits get far more that they paid for, the system is going bankrupt, and the national debt continues to rise dramatically. In other words, totally contrary to the lies being told by Democrats to win votes, the poor and middle class do not pay their fair share of taxes, and the rich pay far more than their fair share. The most vilified top 1% pays about 27% of all federal taxes. That figure is from 2012; it is probably even higher now.

How much federal taxes are actually paid by the rich, the middle class, and the poor? The lowest 20% (average income $15,900) earn 4% of the national income but pay only 1% of the taxes. The second 20% (average income $37,400) earn 8% of the income but pay only 4% of the taxes. The third 20% (average income $58,500) earn 13% of the income but pay only 9% of the taxes. The fourth 20% (average income $85,200) earn 20% of the income and pay 17% of the taxes. The next 10% (average income $120,700) earn 14% of the income and pay 14% of the taxes. The next 5% (average income $161,100) earn 10% of the income and pay 11% of the taxes. The next 4% (average income $277,200) earn 13% of the income but pay 17% of the taxes. The top 1% (average income 1,558,500) earn 18% of the income but pay 27% of the taxes. In other words, the bottom 60% of Americans pay much less than their share of federal taxes (14%), and the greatly and vilified top 1% pay far more than their share (27%).[143]

The foregoing only considers federal income tax. When you consider all taxes paid by Americans i.e. state and local income taxes, real estate taxes, sales taxes, fuel taxes, and all other taxes, then the poor and middle class Americans pay more than above, and wealthy Americans pay far more.

WEALTHY AMERICANS. Democrats have continually stated or implied that wealthy Americans are somehow immoral or unethical because they did not really earn their wealth and do not pay their fair share of taxes. Americans should ask themselves whether Abraham, Job, and King Solomon, all extremely wealthy, were wealthy because they were dishonest or evil, or because they were obedient to God's laws and God's will, found favor with God, and were richly blessed by God.

---

[143] Catherine Mulbrandon, "How Much Taxes Are Paid by the Poor, Middle Class and Rich," VisualizingEconomics, February 2, 2012, http://visualizingeconomics.com/2010/02/12/. Source of figures is Congressional Budget Office most recent figures (2005), http://www.cbo.gov/ftpdocs/88xx/doc8885/EffectiveTaxRates.shtml.

Most wealthy men earn their money lawfully. They know how to make money, and they know how to use money to make more money. The DOW more than doubled in value during the past 8 years, and the real estate market has greatly improved. Many wealthy Americans know how to take advantage of these opportunities to multiply their money. There is absolutely nothing ethically or legally wrong with trying to multiply money through wise investments.

CONCLUSION. During 2016 Hillary Clinton and during 2012 President Obama and other Democrats have made it clear that they want to raise taxes on the "rich" to force them to pay their fair share to relieve the unfair tax burden on the "middle class." Why is this wrong? First, about 49% of Americans, mostly middle and lower class, do not pay any federal taxes. In other words, they are not paying their fair share of taxes.

Also, the U.S. Constitution makes the federal government a government of enumerated powers, where each branch only has those powers which are granted to it by the Constitution. There is absolutely no part of the Constitution that authorizes the social programs which now comprise most of the federal budget. Reduction or elimination of these programs would permit much lower tax rates and make it possible to eliminate the federal deficit and federal debt.

So how could federal tax laws be improved to ensure more "fairness" in taxation of all Americans? One option would be a flat tax where all Americans pay the exact same rate. Most tax deductions and tax credits would be eliminated for all income levels. This would ensure that everyone paid their fair share and would greatly reduce tax fraud, tax preparation time, and the size, cost and workload of the Internal Revenue Service. A second but much more likely option would be to maintain current tax rates but eliminate most tax deductions and tax credits for all tax brackets. This would reduce tax fraud, tax preparation time, and the job of the Internal Revenue Service. A third but much less likely option would be to totally eliminate the federal income tax and totally fund the federal government with sales taxes. This would eliminate the need to complete a federal tax return and greatly reduce tax fraud and the size, cost and function of the Internal Revenue Service.

CHAPTER 8.4

DEMOCRATIC PLATFORM

INTRODUCTION. A new Democratic Platform is published every four years. The 2012 Democratic Platform is a 63-page document that was published in 2012. The 2016 platform is a 55-page document that was published July 21, 2016. This chapter discusses the heart of the 2012 platform first, and then compares the 2016 platform, showing that the heart of the platform remains the same. Readers who do not want to read all the details in this lengthy chapter may jump to the chapter's conclusion for a quick summary.

When reading quotes from the platforms, ask the following questions: (1) Are the statements regarding Republicans, taxes, and other "facts" true? (2) Are the policies Constitutional? (3) Are the policies in agreement with laws and principles given by God through Scripture? As a Christian attorney, I was absolutely shocked by the degree to which the heart of Democratic Platform relies upon lies and deception. But do not take my word. Read it carefully. Verify every fact. Decide for yourself who is speaking the truth. Then read the Constitution; it is not long or complicated. Ask yourself, "Exactly what part of the Constitution grants authority for this policy or program?" Read chapter on Constitution and refer to full text of the Constitution, attached as an Appendix.

2012 DEMOCRATIC PLATFORM. The heart of the 2012 and 2016 Democratic Platforms is the same. The 2012 Democratic Platform states:

Reclaiming the economic security of the middle class is the challenge we must overcome today. That begins by restoring the basic values that made our country great, and restoring for everyone who works hard and plays by the rules the opportunity to find a job that pays the bills, turn an idea into a profitable business, care for your family, afford a home you call your own and health care you can count on, retire with dignity and respect, and, most of all, give your children the kind of education that allows them to dream even bigger and go even further than you ever imagined.

This has to be our North Star—an economy that's built not from the top down, but from a growing middle class, and that provides ladders of opportunity for those working hard to join the middle class.

This is not another trivial political argument. It's the defining issue of our time and at the core of the American Dream. And now we stand at a make-or-break moment, and are faced with a choice between moving forward and falling back.[144]

    CORE ISSUE. These paragraphs make it clear that this issue, which is built on lies and deception as shown below and throughout this book, is the core issue of the Democrats. It is their "North Star." It is "not another trivial political argument."

---

[144] 2012 Democratic Platform, page 2, https://www.democrats.org/party-platform, downloaded 2/2/2016.

It is the "defining issue of our time and the core of the American Dream." In other words, the core issue of the Democratic Party is built on absolute lies about Republicans and the totally false claim that Democrats want equal opportunity for all Americans.

ECONOMIC SECURITY OF MIDDLE CLASS. What could possibly be wrong with the noble goal of "reclaiming the economic security of the middle class?" First, God forbids discrimination based on class or wealth. Exodus states, "Do not show favoritism to a poor person in a lawsuit" (Ex 23: 3). Leviticus states, "Do not pervert justice; do not show partiality to the poor or favoritism to the great, but judge your neighbor fairly" (Lev 19:15, NIV). Job declares that God "shows no partiality to princes and does not favor the rich over the poor, for they are all the work of his hands?" (Job 34: 19). That is why God's "tax rate" was exactly the same for the rich and the poor: 10%. See chapter on taxes.

Second, the Declaration of Independence states that: (1) God creates all men equal; (2) with "certain unalienable Rights that [...include] Life, Liberty and the pursuit of Happiness;" (3) "to secure these rights, Governments are instituted among Men." This clearly implies that all men are created equal and entitled to equal and fair treatment under the law, and that the responsibility of government is to ensure equal and fair treatment under the law. Protecting the right to "the pursuit of happiness" requires that the government protect every man's right to keep and spend money that he has lawfully earned, to enable his "pursuit of happiness."

Third, the Constitution does not grant any power, jurisdiction, or authority to any branch of the government to discriminate for or against any group of citizens based upon their class, wealth, or any other factor. The Founding Fathers never discriminated for or against any group based on class or wealth.

Fourth: "That the Commonwealth may be a nation of laws, and not of men." These words, inscribed in very large letters on the full length of the north side of the main courthouse in Cincinnati, Ohio, clearly state one of the most important principles that our nation was founded upon. The United States is governed by laws that apply to all men equally. It is not governed by men who have the right or freedom to show favoritism to the rich, poor, middle class, or any other class or group of citizens.

Fifth, it is not ethical or legal for a poor man to put a gun to the head of a rich man and take his money. It is also not ethical for the government to do the same thing, to forcefully take lawfully earned money from a rich man and give it to a poor man. The end does not justify the means.

Sixth, Democrats falsely claim that they want equal opportunity for all Americans. They want discrimination based upon class. They falsely claim that the "rich" or "the wealthy few" are not paying their "fair share" of taxes; the opposite is true. They falsely imply that the "middle class" are paying more than their fair share of taxes; the opposite is true. They falsely imply that if the "rich" or "the wealthy few" pay their "fair share" of taxes, that the additional money taken from them can be used to restore equal opportunity to the "middle class" through government programs that give educational, healthcare, and other benefits.

Democrats continually want to keep raising taxes on the rich to enable transfer of their money to federal programs that create opportunities for the poor and middle class. Even when most of the poor and middle class pay no taxes and even when the rich pay a far greater percentage, it is never enough. No matter how little the poor and middle class pay and no matter how much the rich pay, to win votes Democrats will always promise to take money from the rich and give it to the poor and middle class. So Democrats vote for whoever promises them the most financial benefit in the form of government benefits. Basically, they are voting to have the government forcefully take money from "rich" Americans and give it to them.

RESTORING BASIC VALUES. Republicans would completely agree with the second sentence in the quote from the Democratic Platform, "restoring the basic values that made our country great, and restoring for everyone who works hard and plays by the rules" all the opportunities that they deserve. However, Republicans would say that this can only be achieved by treating all Americans equally under the law, by having no discrimination based on class, wealth, or any other factor. Democrats do not want the equality of opportunity that they claim they want. They want discrimination based upon class and economic standing. That is why they are always talking about class. Again, the federal government has absolutely no authority, jurisdiction, or power under God's law or the Constitution to discriminate in any way based upon class or economic standing. It has a duty to apply the law equally to all citizens.

One must choose between equality of opportunity and equality of results; it is impossible to strive for both at the same time. Republicans and Democrats are in total agreement that all Americans should have equality of opportunity. However, Democrats are being totally dishonest when they claim that they want equality of opportunity for all Americans. They want discrimination based upon class or economic standing to achieve equality of results. President Obama, talking about the rich, said, "You didn't earn that!" Democrats have the attitude that the rich do not deserve the money they have, even if it was earned lawfully by work or investments.

"Restoring the basic values that made our country great" would require going back to the government policies of a time when the federal government did not offer any educational, healthcare, or other financial benefits to citizens. Politicians were not able to buy votes with promises of money in the form of government benefits. Americans had to earn their own money, not look to the government for handouts. The size and role of the federal government was limited to the powers granted to it by the Constitution. Taxes were much lower overall, so more Americans were able to keep and spend more of their own money.

LIES ABOUT REPUB LICANS. The Democratic Platform contains many lies about the Republican Party. It states:

> The Republican Party has turned its back on the middle class Americans who built this country. Our opponents believe we should go back to the top-down economic policies of the last decade. They think that if we simply eliminate protections for families and consumers, let Wall Street write its own rules again, and cut taxes for the wealthiest, the market will solve all our problems on its own. They argue that if we help corporations and wealthy investors maximize

180

their profits by whatever means necessary, whether through layoffs or outsourcing, it will automatically translate into jobs and prosperity that benefits us all. They would repeal health reform, turn Medicare into a voucher program, and follow the same path of fiscal irresponsibility of the past administration— giving trillions of dollars in tax cuts weighted towards millionaires and billionaires while sticking the middle class with the bill. But we've tried their policies—and we've all suffered when they failed.[145]

It is not enough to go back to where the country was before the crisis. We must rebuild a strong foundation that ensures it never happens again.

First and foremost, every single statement about Republicans in this section of the Democratic Platform is totally and absolutely false. The amazing magnitude of the dishonesty of Democrats is proven by the words in this section.

Commentary on "Republican Party has turned its back on the middle class"and going "back to the top-down economic policies of the last decade back to the top-down economic policies of the last decade." The Republican Party never turned its back on the middle class. They never wanted to "eliminate protections for families and consumers, let Wall Street write its own rules again, and cut taxes for the wealthiest." The exact opposite is true. Between 2008 and 2012 a Republican Congress increased the tax rates for the

---

[145] 2012 Democratic Platform, page 2, https://www.democrats.org/party-platform, downloaded 2/2/2016

"wealthiest" Americans from 35% to 39.6%. For countless years, Republicans have joined forces with Democrats to establish tax rates and credits and deductions which greatly favor the poor and middle class. See chapter on Taxation for details.

No Democrat ever heard any Republican "argue that if we help corporations and wealthy investors maximize their profits by whatever means necessary, whether through layoffs or outsourcing, it will automatically translate into jobs and prosperity that benefits us all." No Republican ever said this. So why is the Democratic Platform filled with so many statements that are such blatant lies? The answer is simply that the lies are believed by voters.

Commentary on "repeal health form" and "turn Medicare into a voucher program." No Republican running for president has advocated turning Medicare into a voucher program." The federal government has absolutely no jurisdiction, power, or authority to implement a national healthcare program. See chapter on healthcare for detailed discussion. However, Americans have paid taxes to support Medicare and therefore deserve to receive the Medicare benefits that they paid for; therefore both Republicans and Democrats want to keep and support Medicare.

Commentary on "follow the same path of fiscal irresponsibility of the past administration—giving trillions of dollars in tax cuts weighted towards millionaires and billionaires while sticking the middle class with the bill." Again, these statements are totally and absolutely false. The exact opposite is true. For countless years, Republicans have joined forces with Democrats to establish tax rates and credits and deductions which greatly favor the poor and middle class. A Republican Congress just increased the tax rates for the "wealthiest" Americans. See chapter on Taxation for details. The Democratic Platform keeps repeating these false accusations because they are key parts of the foundation of the Democratic Platform.

EQUAL OPPORTUNITY FOR ALL AMERICANS. The Democratic Platform goes on to state some noble objectives.

> Democrats know that America prospers when we're all in it together. We see an America where everyone has a fair shot, does their fair share, and plays by the same rules. We see an America that out-educates, out-builds, and out-innovates the rest of the world.

Republicans would be in full agreement with all of these statements. They agree that "America prospers when we're all in it together." They want " an America where everyone has a fair shot, does their fair share, and plays by the same rules…an America that out-educates, out-builds, and out-innovates the rest of the world." However, Democrats do not want an America where everyone "plays by the same rules." They want discrimination based upon class and wealth. Democrats do not want an America where everyone "does their fair share." They want to give government benefits to those who have not earned them, a transfer of money from those who have earned it lawfully to those who have not earned it.

END NOT JUSTIFY MEANS. The Democratic Platform states great goals for America, but the end does not justify the means.

We see an America with greater economic security and opportunity, driven by education, energy, innovation and infrastructure, and a tax code that helps to create American jobs and bring down the debt in a balanced way. We believe in deficit reduction not by placing the burden on the middle class and the poor, but by cutting out programs we can't afford and asking the wealthiest to again contribute their fair share.[146]

Republicans would agree with everything in this paragraph except the discrimination based upon wealth or class. Consider the absolute absurdity, impossibility, and extreme dishonesty of Democrats who in this passage say they do not want to ask the poor or middle class to do anything to help reduce the national deficit. They only want the "wealthiest to again contribute their fair share." They also say that they want to cut "programs we can't afford." But they are the ones who always want more programs and bigger programs to do a better job of caring for the poor and the middle class. And at the same time that their platform states that they want to cut programs to reduce the deficit, under President Obama they have introduced Obamacare, one of the most expensive programs in the history of the United States, a program that will cost as much as the United States remaining at war for the remainder of its history.

DIFFERENT VISIONS. The Democratic Platform gives a very false impression of the different visions of Republican and Democrats.

---

[146] 2012 Democratic Platform, page 2, https://www.democrats.org/party-platform, downloaded 2/2/2016

We Democrats offer America the opportunity to move our country forward by creating an economy built to last and built from the middle out. Mitt Romney and the Republican Party have a drastically different vision. They still believe the best way to grow the economy is from the top down—the same approach that benefited the wealthy few but crashed the economy and crushed the middle class."[147]

Again, every statement about Republicans is an absolute lie. The Republican Party does not want to "grow the economy from the top down." Republicans want grow the economy by ensuring equal opportunity for all Americans, by not discriminating against anyone on the basis of class or anything else. Democrats want discrimination based upon class. That is why they are always talking about class.

Democrats falsely imply that Republicans implemented policies that "benefited the wealthy few but crashed the economy and crushed the middle class." Republicans did not advance policies that "benefited the wealth few" and they did not advance any policies that crashed the economy or crushed the middle class. The primary reason that the economy crashed is that mortgages were given to so many people who should not have qualified and who then defaulted. The federal regulations that enabled less financially qualified individuals to obtain mortgages were signed into law by a Democrat, President Clinton, not President Bush.

2016 DEMOCRATIC PLATFORM. Quotes from the

---

[147] 2012 Democratic Platform, page 2, https://www.democrats.org/party-platform, downloaded 2/2/2016.

2016 platform show that the same false statements and promises are being made in 2016. The 2016 Democratic Platform begins by citing the accomplishments of the Obama Administration. It falsely states that Republican policies triggered the Great Recession. Again, it was President Clinton, who simply wanted to make home ownership more affordable to more Americans who signed into law regulations which enabled many Americans who never should have qualified for home loans to get mortgages, which led to the economic crash.

> Under President Obama's leadership, and thanks to the hard work and determination of the American people, we have come a long way from the Great Recession and the Republican policies that triggered it. American businesses have now added 14.8 million jobs since private-sector job growth turned positive in early 2010. Twenty million people have gained health insurance coverage. The American auto industry just had its best year ever. And we are getting more of our energy from the sun and wind, and importing less oil from overseas.

The jobs figure fails to note the millions of Americans who are not part of the statistics because they have given up on looking for a job. The health insurance figures fail to consider the insurance companies refusing to continue with Obamacare because they have lost so much money with it (Aetna, etc.) or the simple fact that Constitution does not give any branch of the federal government any authority to institute a national healthcare system. See chapter on Healthcare (Obamacare). The comments about "getting more of our energy from the sun and wind" win votes dishonestly because there is no significant increase in use of energy from the sun or wind.

The next paragraph lists the many problems that "too many Americans" still have after 8 years under the leadership of President Obama.

> But too many Americans have been left out and left behind. They are working longer hours with less security. Wages have barely budged and the racial wealth gap remains wide, while the cost of everything from childcare to a college education has continued to rise. And for too many families, the dream of homeownership is out of reach. As working people struggle, the top one percent accrues more wealth and more power. Republicans in Congress have chosen gridlock and dysfunction over trying to find solutions to the real challenges we face. It's no wonder that so many feel like the system is rigged against them.

So why do so many Americans have so many problems after 8 years under President Obama? Why should Americans vote for Hillary Clinton if she will continue the policies of the Obama Administration? The Democratic Platform does not answer these questions or take any responsibility for the fact that "too many Americans have been left out and left behind." Instead, as always, it dishonestly blames the rich ("top one percent") and Republicans.

Totally contrary to the false claims of Democrats, Americans are not victims of the wealthy or Republicans. This entire book reveals the moral depravity of Democratic principles and policies, and shows that Republican principles and policies are much more in line with God's principles and laws embodied in scripture, the Declaration of Independence, the Constitution, and the Bill of Rights. Also, as stated in the chapter on Truth on Taxes, the top one percent already pays about 27% of all federal taxes, much more than their fair share. And about half of Americans, mostly middle class, do not pay any federal taxes, so they are the ones who do not pay their fair share for national defense, the roads they travel on, etc.

The next paragraph contains more false statements and again presents the same totally wrong, unethical, solution that Democrats always present i.e. taking more money from the rich and giving it to the middle class.

> We will <u>ensure those at the top contribute to our country's future by establishing a multimillionaire surtax to ensure millionaires and billionaires pay their fair share</u>. In addition, we will shut down the "private tax system" for those at the top, immediately close egregious loopholes like those enjoyed by hedge fund managers, restore fair taxation on multimillion dollar estates, and ensure millionaires can no longer pay a lower rate than their secretaries. At a time of near-record corporate profits, slow wage growth, and rising costs, we need to offer <u>tax relief to middle-class families—not those at the top.</u>

First, the next president cannot lawfully and will not establish "a multimillionaire surtax" to force the most wealthy to pay higher taxes. That is a lie designed to win votes. Also, there is no "private tax system" for those at the top. That is another lie designed to win votes. Every statement in this paragraph is a lie designed to win votes. Also, note that after eight years of having President Obama in office, Democrats are still trying to win votes with the same false promise of "tax relief to the middle-class families—not those at the top" based upon the same false claim that the rich are not paying their fair share of taxes and the middle class are paying more than their fair share.

> We will offer tax relief to hard working, middle-class families for the cost squeeze they have faced for years from rising health care, childcare, education, and other expenses. Donald Trump and the Republican Party would do the opposite and provide trillions in tax cuts for millionaires, billionaires, and corporations at the expense of working families, seniors, and the health of our economy.

Again, Democrats make the same totally false statements about Republicans, claiming that they want to give millions in tax cuts to the rich at the expense of "working families and seniors. That is totally false. They repeat the same lies because they work, because they win votes.

CONCLUSION. Now consider exactly how Democrats try to win votes. Consider the absolute impossibility of paying for the long list of government benefits that they promise. They promise to "everyone who works hard and plays by the rules the opportunity to find a job that pays the bills, turn an idea into a profitable business, care for your family, afford a home you call your own and health care you can count on, retire with dignity and respect, and, most of all, give your children the kind of education that allows them to dream even bigger and go even further than you ever imagined." They promise tuition-free college, healthcare for all Americans, Social Security, Medicaid and/or Medicare, etc. They promise to provide all these benefits and to reduce the national deficit by only raising taxes on the "wealthy few."

In other words, Democrats promise to provide the majority of Americans with a very long list of extremely costly benefits and reduce the deficit without any cost to the vast majority of Americans, by only making the wealthiest pay their "fair share." Again, the claim that the wealthy few are not paying their fair share of taxes is an absolute lie. The opposite is true; they pay more than their fair share. Democrats falsely imply that the "middle class" are paying more than their fair share of taxes. Again, the opposite is true; many pay absolutely no federal taxes. See chapter on Taxes.

CHAPTER 9.0

VOTING OTHER ISSUES

SECTION REVIEW. Christians should NOT vote first based upon any of the issues discussed in this section except national security and terrorism. Christians should vote first based upon God's laws and principles revealed through scripture. Christians should vote second based upon laws and principles embodied in the Declaration of Independence, Constitution, and Bill of Rights. One of these issues is national security and terrorism, because the President, as Commander in Chief, is responsible for protection of all Americans from "all enemies foreign and domestic." All other issues discussed in this section should be given lower priority.

CHAPTERS:
9.1 National Security and Terrorism
9.2 Jobs and the Economy
9.3 Immigration
9.4 Healthcare (Obamacare)
9.5 Education
9.6 Climate Change and Environment

NATIONAL DEFENSE AND TERRORISM

INTRODUCTION. The primary and most important constitutional duty of the President is to serve as Commander in Chief of all armed forces of the United States and to defend Americans from "all enemies, foreign and domestic." This chapter discusses national defense in general, and the current threat of domestic and international terrorism.

NATIONAL DEFENSE—TOP PRIORITY. Most Republicans and Democrats running for president claim they will do the best job of defending America. So who is more truthful? Who can be trusted to do the best job of protecting Americans? Most Americans know that the first and foremost priority of Republican presidents is to serve as Commander in Chief and to defend America from all enemies foreign and domestic. They also know the top priority of Democrats is not national defense, but taking care of Americans through totally unconstitutional costly healthcare and education programs. See chapter on Democratic Platform for discussion of programs.

NATIONAL DEFENSE—FUNDING. Democrats have a history of reducing funding of the military to fund their social programs. Republicans have a history of better funding and support of our armed forces, and better defense of our nation from all enemies, both foreign and domestic.

COMMANDER IN CHIEF—TEAM LEADER. Although the President serves as Commander in Chief, national defense is not a one-man job. It requires building and working with teams i.e. National Security Council, Joint Chief of Staffs, Secretaries of Army, Navy, Air Force, etc. Trump has excellent team-building skills, witnessed by all Americans on television. Clinton has not demonstrated team-building skills, and was overstressed and had health problems due to exhaustion from trying to be Secretary of State.

COMMMANDER IN CHIEF—WISDOM AND LOYALTY. Hillary Clinton has proven that she could not be trusted to exercise common sense in safeguarding her emails as Secretary of State. If she did not have the simple, common sense to safeguard top-level U.S. government communications, how can she be expected to have the wisdom needed to safeguard our nation? Trump can be trusted to build the better teams, such as the National Security Council, to seek their counsel, and to thereby exercise greater wisdom as Commander in Chief in defending Americans from all enemies, foreign and domestic.

Hillary Clinton betrayed all Americans by compromising our national security interests in exchange for donations to the Clinton Fund and millions of dollars paid to her husband for speeches. She gave Russia 20% of U.S. uranium production, a very rare element needed for our own nuclear power plants and nuclear weapons. She gave U.S. nuclear technology to India.

TERRORISM—ISIS/ISIL. One of the greatest threats to the United State is domestic and international terrorism. The greatest terrorist threat to the United States and Europe in 2016 is posed by ISIS/ISIL. What are these groups and what is the difference between ISIS and ISIL?

The two acronyms refer to the same group. ISIS stands for Islamic State in Iraq and Syria because the group's territory straddles the border between the two counties. ISIL stands for Islamic State in Iraq and the Levant. The Levant is the historic name given to the entire region east of the Mediterranean from Egypt, east to Iran and to Turkey. U.S. officials use ISIL instead of ISIS to emphasize the group's goal to expand its influence beyond the borders of Syria and Iraq. The group began as a splinter from the terrorist group al Qaeda. The goal of ISIS is to create an Islamic state in Middle Eastern and African countries."[148]

Donald Trump has demonstrated much greater concern for and dedication to defeating ISIS/ISIL overseas, in Syria, Iraq, etc. Hillary Clinton gives higher priority to a host of domestic issues for which the president has no constitutional authority (education, healthcare, etc.).

DOMESTIC TERRORISM. During the past few years, domestic terrorism has repeatedly posed a threat to Americans. President Obama said the terrorist threat has "evolved into a new phase" of attacks hatched at home by extremists "poisoning the minds" of killers already on American soil.[149] Many Americans have been killed or injured on American soil by fellow Americans inspired by foreign terrorists. Donald Trump has demonstrated much greater concern and dedication to defeating terrorism on American soil. He has also promised to build a better wall between Mexico and the United States, which will more effectively prevent any foreign terrorists from entering the United States.

CONCLUSION. Hillary Clinton, like other Democrats,

---

[148] "ISIS vs ISIL—what's the difference?" Kacie Yearout, USA Today Network, December 29, 2015.
[149] Ibid.

cannot be trusted to make national security or funding of the armed forces of the United States her top priority. Her top priority is taking care of Americans through costly, totally unconstitutional social programs outlined in the Democratic Platform (education, healthcare, etc.). Only Trump can be trusted to make national defense his top priority, to restore military strength, and to properly defend Americans from all enemies, foreign and domestic.

JOBS AND THE ECONOMY

INTRODUCTION. Jobs and the economy are a primary consideration when voting for many Americans. However, the Constitution gives the President limited power to influence jobs and the economy. His primary job is to protect the rights, freedom, and security of Americans to enable jobs and the economy to prosper.

THE CLINTONS. In 1992 Bill Clinton used the words, "It's the economy, stupid," to belittle then President Herbert W. Bush (father of President George W. Bush), and to convince voters that he would do a better job of getting them jobs and restoring the national economy. What is amazing is that Bill Clinton, as the Governor of the state of Arkansas, was less qualified to deal with jobs and the economy on a national level than President Bush, who had years of experience as President. But Clinton's advisors knew that insulting and belittling the President would win the support of voters.

Fast forward to 2016. Hillary Clinton actually said that she will put her husband in charge of the economy. Do Americans really want a President who puts her husband in charge of the economy? Is she so ignorant regarding jobs and the economy that she would simply put her husband in charge that vitally important area? The answer is yes--she has virtually no education, experience, or expertise in the area of jobs and the economy.

TRUMP. Donald Trump has much more than an academic degree from a top business school. He has countless years of experience in the business world, much more than any other president in the history of the United States. He would be the most knowledgeable and most experienced President when it comes to the business world, jobs, and the economy.

Hillary Clinton has falsely warned Americans that Donald Trump would bankrupt the United States, because he repeatedly declared bankruptcy. Donald Trump knows the rules and laws that govern business, and has used them to become extremely wealthy. He would apply that same knowledge, experience, and expertise to improving jobs and the economy for all Americans.

Americans have witnessed the business acumen of Donald Trump at work on the television show "The Apprentice." They have witnessed his discernment and skill in putting together teams to tackle assigned projects. Being President is not a one-man job. It requires team building skills which Trump has proven and Clinton lacks.

Americans who want to more fully understand the incredible business expertise and experience of Donald Trump can read any of his books. These include (1) "Great Again: How to Fix our Crippled America" (2016), (2) "Time to Get Tough: Make America Great Again" (2015), (3) Crippled America: How to Make America Great Again" (2015), (4) "Trump: The Art of the Deal" (2015), (5) "Midas Touch: Why Some Entrepreneurs Get Rich and Why Most Don't" (2012), and (6) "Think Like a Champion: An Informal Education in Business and Life" (2010), (7) "Think Big: Make it Happen in Business and in Life" (2008), and (8) "Trump: How to Get Rich " (2004).

CONCLUSION. Donald Trump is infinitely more qualified to deal with jobs and the economy than Hillary Clinton. Indeed, he would be more qualified than any other President in the history of the United States. He knows how to build teams to help him discharge his responsibilities as President. And he would be outstanding at negotiating better economic, nuclear, military, and other agreements with other nations.

CHAPTER 9.3

IMMIGRATION

INTRODUCTION. Christians should not vote first on immigration. They should vote first based upon God's laws and principles revealed through scripture and second based upon American laws and principles embodied in the Declaration of Independence, Constitution, and Bill of Rights.

TRUMP VS. CLINTON. There are sharp differences between Trump and Clinton on immigration. Everyone knows or should know that Trump will do a better job of protecting Americans from: (1) immigration of terrorists from Syria and other nations, (2) drug traffic from Mexico, and (3) illegal immigration from Mexico. Clinton will place far fewer restrictions on immigration, and is far more likely to legalize millions of illegal immigrants.

IMMIGRATION AND TERRORISM. Most immigrants from Mexico want to live and work in the United States and be law-abiding citizens. Most are Catholics who pose no threat of terrorism to the United States. The same cannot be said for Muslims. ISIS/ISIL terrorists strongly desire to infiltrate immigrants fleeing Syria or other Arab nations and commit acts of terror in the United States and Europe. It would be terrorist malpractice to not try to do so. Democratic candidates claim that we should allow properly vetted immigrants from Syria into the United States. However, it is absolutely impossible to properly vet these immigrants. When I had to get a top-secret clearance in the Army, the Army gathered information on every place that I had lived, worked, and attended school. It is impossible to properly investigate individuals fleeing war-torn Syria. There is no one to call and no way to verify their information or whether or not they pose a threat to the United States.

The Christian values of freedom of speech and freedom of religion are vital parts of the Constitution. The Koran does not permit freedom of religion or freedom of speech. Christians in Egypt are required to pay higher taxes because the Koran requires higher taxes from non-Muslims. Authors in Europe were killed for criticizing Islam. Non-Muslims who try to share their faith in a Muslim nation may be imprisoned. The Bible commands Christians to love their enemies. The Koran offers great reward for killing non-Muslims.

In some Muslim communities in Europe and the United States, Muslims have tried to implement and enforce their laws, which may be totally contrary to state and federal laws. After Germany accepted many thousands of Syrian refugees, crime rates for theft and rape skyrocketed, and Germans are setting new records for the purchase of tasers and other self-defense weapons. There are about 25 Muslim Arab nations. Some are very wealthy. Syrian refugees should be required to flee to these nations, who speak their language and practice their religion.

CONCLUSION. The presidential candidates sharply differ on immigration. Americans who want more protection from immigration of terrorists, illegal drug traffic, and illegal immigration should vote for Trump. Americans who want fewer restrictions on immigration and the legalization of millions of illegal immigrants should vote for Clinton.

CHAPTER 9.4

EDUCATION

INTRODUCTION. No American should vote for any candidate based upon any promise of educational benefits. It is illegal and unethical for any candidate for federal office to promise educational benefits to voters.

DECEPTION TO WIN VOTES. To win votes, Democrats promise generous but totally unconstitutional educational benefits that do not have to paid for by their voters. First, Democrats lie by telling Americans that they have the right to education benefits from the federal government. Each branch of the federal government only has those powers specifically granted to it by the Constitution. The Constitution does not give the president or any other part of the federal government any jurisdiction or authority to grant educational benefits to any American.

Second, Democrats try to convince voters that they have the right to education benefits that they do not have to pay for, that are paid for by other taxpayers. The federal government has no moral right or legal authority to forcefully take lawfully earned income from one taxpayer and use it to pay the education bills of another taxpayer. See chapters on Constitution and Bill of Rights.

2016 ELECTION. During the 2016 election, Hillary Clinton and Democrats offered free college education to all families who earn less than $125,000/year (83% of all families) and debt free education to all others. Clinton promised to pay for all this by only increasing taxes on the richest Americans and on corporations. She falsely claimed that rich were not paying their fair share. The rich are already paying virtually all federal income taxes. The top 1% is already paying about 27% of all federal income taxes. US corporations already pay some of the highest corporate taxes in the world. Our College debt already exceeds credit card debt in the United States. Obama has doubled the national debt without giving free college. There is absolutely no way that Democrats can pay for all the educational benefits that they have promised to voters, but they know that they can win votes with their false promises.

CONCLUSION. No American should vote for any Democrat who promises unconstitutional federal educational benefits. It is illegal and immoral to forcefully take money from some taxpayers and give it to others in the form of educational benefits. It is also absolutely impossible for Democrats to pay for the very generous educational benefits that they have promised to voters.

CHAPTER 9.5

HEALTHCARE (OBAMACARE)

INTRODUCTION. On March 23, 2010, President Obama "signed the Patient Protection and Affordable Care Act (Obamacare) into law, which will provide federal funding for health plans that pay for abortion on demand and lead to large-scale rationing of lifesaving medical treatments."[150]

Governor Romney said, "Obamacare will violate that crucial first principle of medicine" 'Do no harm.'"[151] He believes the Obama health care law, which would open the door to federal subsidies for abortion coverage and rationing of lifesaving medical care, should be repealed.[152]

RESULTS OF OBAMACARE. Exactly what are the results or consequences of Obamacare for Christians?

1. ABORTION. "Obamacare is a massive expansion of taxpayer-subsidized abortion.[153] In other words, American

---

[150] "National Right to Life Endorses Governor Mitt Romney," "Where Do the Candidates Stand on Life: Mitt Romney, Barack Obama," Carol Tobias, "Statement by Carol Tobias, National Right to Life President," April 12, 2012, State Senate," National Right to Life, Committee, http://www.nrlc.org.
[151] "Where Do the Candidates Stand on Life: Mitt Romney, Barack Obama."
[152] "National Right to Life Endorses Governor Mitt Romney" and Carol Tobias, "Statement by Carol Tobias, National Right to Life President."
[153] Bruce Hausknecht, "Obamacare Decision Next Week: What's at Stake?", June 22, 2012, http://www.citizenlink.com. See Citizenlink website at http://www.citizenlink.com/2012/10/29/pro-life-group-proves-that-obamacare-subsidizes-abortion/.

taxpayers who believe that abortion is murder are forced to pay higher taxes to fund millions of abortions. After describing in great detail President Obama's very lengthy and "abysmal record on life,"[154] Carol Tobias, President of National Right to Life, said,

But even more far-reaching than all of this, is how the president is impacting our health care system. In 2012, Congress passed and President Obama signed into law, the Patient Protection and Affordable Care Act, also known as ObamaCare. Today, every fifth child dies from abortion; that number will go even higher because of ObamaCare. This program will enshrine abortion and rationing of health care in our society for generations to come if it isn't stopped.[155]

2. RELIGIOUS FREEDOM. The mandate from the Health and Human Services (different from individual mandate to buy insurance), a byproduct of Obamacare, "requires most religious organizations and their private employers to provide employee healthcare coverage for drugs, medical procedures and other services against their deeply held religious beliefs."[156] These drugs and medical procedures may include abortion, abortion inducing drugs, contraceptives, sterilization, reproductive counseling, etc.[157] Andy Newland, Vice President of Hercules Industries, said the mandate requires business owners to compromise their beliefs.

---

[154] Carol Tobias, "Statement by Carol Tobias, National Right to Life President."
[155] Ibid.
[156] Bruce Hausknecht, "Obamacare Decision Next Week: What's at Stake?"
[157] Bethany Monk, "HHS Contraception Mandate Deadline Falls Wednesday," July 31, 2012, http://www.citizenlink.com; "President Obama to Freedom of Religion: Nertz to You!", Family Reseach Council Action, August 6, 2012, http://www.frcaction.org.

We never imagined the federal government would order our family business to provide insurance for drugs we object to covering. If you put yourself back to when the Founders founded America, it seems so contradictory to their intention that Americans be free to live out their beliefs in a country that was created for freedom from religious persecution.[158]

Newland said the mandate prevents families from bringing their moral and principles into their business. "What ethical and moral principles do you use to run your business? We'll end up with no ethical or moral principals at all."[159]

Emily Hardman, Communications Director for Becket Fund for Religious Liberty, said that the mandate is "a violation of those individuals with religious beliefs… People don't have to give up their faith when they enter their business."[160]

The only organizations exempted from the mandate are seminaries and churches that only employ and serve members of their own faith (and plans "grandfathered" under the rule). Catholic universities and hospitals are not exempt.[161] They are forced to violate their deeply held religious beliefs.

Fines for non-compliance can be as much as $100 per day per employee, an amount that can bankrupt a business.[162] In other words, to survive in the United States, Christian businesses or organizations will be forced by the government to violate their deeply held moral and religious beliefs.

---

[158] Ibid.
[159] Ibid.
[160] Ibid.
[161] Ibid.
[162] "President Obama to Freedom of Religion: Nertz to You!"

3. LIMITS ON GOVERNMENT. The "individual mandate" of Obamacare (different from mandate of Health and Human Services) requires all Americans to buy health insurance or pay a penalty.[163] This mandate is totally contrary to the U.S. Constitution, the highest law of our nation, as explained below.

4. COST TO TAXPAYERS. The incredibly high cost of Obamacare to U.S. taxpayers will continue to rise dramatically. In 2010 the Congressional Budget Office estimated the ten-year cost of Obamacare to be $944 billion. In 2011 it estimated $1,442 billion. In 2012 it estimated $1,856 billion. See Forbes Magazine article at footnote.[164]

5. COST TO STATES. Obamacare requires states to demand "massive dollars" from taxpayers to fund Obamacare. States must raise $33.5 billion from 2014 to 2020.[165]

6. REDISTRIBUTION OF WEALTH. Obamacare is a massive, monumental federal redistribution of wealth program that any good socialist or communist would take great pride in having created. Totally contrary to the U.S. Constitution, it forces American taxpayers to pay the healthcare bills of other Americans. How massive is the redistribution? The Los Angeles Times reports that California will receive about $15 billion from American taxpayers.[166] How would you feel if the government forced you to pay for

---

[163] Bruce Hausknecht, "Obamacare Decision Next Week: What's at Stake?"
[164] Avik Roy, "CBO: Obamacare Will Spend More, Tax More, and Reduce the Deficit Less Than We Previously Thought," August 27, 2012, http://www.forbes.com.
[165] Bruce Hausknecht, "Obamacare Decision Next Week: What's at Stake?"
[166] Ibid.

all the healthcare bills of your neighbors? How can any elected or appointed government official be so incredibly stupid to think that healthcare is a right, and that the government has the right to force any American to pay the healthcare bills of other Americans? What about the food bills, the rent or mortgage bills, the home heating bills, the college education bills, the legal bills, etc. Exactly where do you draw the line and why?

U.S. CONSTITUTION. Question: Exactly what part of the U.S. Constitution mentions healthcare and gives the federal government authority to legislate national healthcare? Answer: Absolutely no part. The federal government of the United States is a government of enumerated powers. Each branch of government only has the powers granted to it by the Constitution. All other powers are reserved to the states. Healthcare is not even mentioned in the Constitution. The federal government has absolutely no authority to enact national healthcare.

Exactly what part of the Constitution is wrongfully used to justify legislation regarding many subject areas not even mentioned in the Constitution? Answer: The Interstate Commerce Clause. Article 1, Section 8, states: "The Congress shall have Power…To regulate Commerce with foreign Nations, and among the several States, and with the Indian Tribes."[167] The author of this book used the nation's most popular bar-preparation materials to prepare for the bar examination that enabled him to practice law. The law professor advising law school graduates throughout the United States said, "If you have any question about whether or not the

---

[167] Constitution of the United States, U.S. National Archives & Records Administration, 8601 Adelphi Road, College Park, MD, 20740-6001, • 1-86-NARA-NARA • 1-866-272-6272; http://www.archives.gov/exhibits/charters/constitution.html.

Interstate Commerce Clause authorizes the federal government to do something, the answer is: 'Yes!'" In other words, the federal government wrongfully uses the Interstate Commerce Clause to justify legislation in many areas not authorized by the Constitution.

SUPREME COURT RULING. On June 28, 2012 the United States Supreme Court ruled Obamacare to be constitutional. Justice Kennedy was expected to be the deciding vote between liberals and conservatives. However, in a shocking turn of events that surprised even the experts, Chief Justice Roberts, a conservative appointed by President George W. Bush, joined four liberal justices in ruling Obamacare constitutional. Neither Justice Kennedy nor the conservative justices were able to convince Chief Justice Roberts to rejoin conservatives in ruling Obamacare unconstitutional. To see entire text of 193-page majority opinion, go to reference in footnote.[168]

SCOTUS stands for Supreme Court of the United States. SCOTUSblog is sponsored by Bloomberg Law. SCOTUSblog summarized the majority opinion of the Affordable Care Act in one paragraph.

> In Plain English: The Affordable Care Act, including its individual mandate that virtually all Americans buy health insurance, is constitutional. There were not five votes to uphold it on the ground that Congress could use its power to regulate commerce between the states to require everyone to buy health insurance. However, five

---

[168] "The Supreme Court's Obamacare Decision: Full Text," The Atlantic, June 28, 2012, http://www.theatlantic.com/politics/archive/2012/06/the-supreme-courts-obamacare-decision-full-text/259102/.

Justices agreed that the penalty that someone must pay if he refuses to buy insurance is a kind of tax that Congress can impose using its taxing power. That is all that matters. Because the mandate survives, the Court did not need to decide what other parts of the statute were constitutional, except for a provision that required states to comply with new eligibility requirements for Medicaid or risk losing their funding. On that question, the Court held that the provision is constitutional as long as states would only lose new funds if they didn't comply with the new requirements, rather than all of their funding.[169]

In an article entitled "Roberts: Our Decision Isn't About Whether Obamacare Is Sound Policy," Chief Justice Roberts explained the ruling upholding the Affordable Care Act:

We do not consider whether the Act embodies sound policies. That judgment is entrusted to the Nation's elected leaders. We ask only whether Congress has the power under the Constitution to enact the challenged provisions. In this case we must again determine whether the Constitution grants Congress powers it now asserts, but which many States and individuals believe it does not possess. Resolving this controversy requires us to examine both the limits of the Government's power, and our own limited role in policing those

---

[169] Derek Thompson, "The Health Care Decision Explained in 1 Paragraph on SCOTUSblog," The Atlantic, June 28, 2012, http://www.theatlantic.com/business/archive/2012/06/the-health-care-decision-explained-in-1-paragraph-on-scotusblog/259097/.

boundaries. [170]

In other words, Chief Justice Roberts first and foremost made it abundantly clear that his decision did not mean that he approved of the legislation by Congress as good policy for the nation. That was the responsibility of elected members of Congress. The question remains: Why did Chief Justice John Roberts decide to join liberal justices in ruling Obamacare constitutional? The Catholic World News explained his decision as follows:

> The US Supreme Court has upheld the constitutionality of President Obama's sweeping health-care reform legislation. Writing for the majority in a hotly contested 5-4 decision, Chief Justice John Roberts said that the individual mandate—the requirement that every citizen must purchase health insurance—was in effect a tax. "Because the Constitution permits such a tax, it is not our role to forbid it, or to pass upon its wisdom or fairness," he wrote.
> The June 28 ruling does not affect the lawsuits brought by Catholic institutions to challenge the law's requirement that all health-care insurance programs must include coverage for contraception. Those suits will continue to move forward. The US bishops' conference responded to the Supreme Court decision by urging Congress to change the law, saying that it should be amended to eliminate funding for abortion, ensure conscience rights, and

---

[170] Chief Justice Roberts, "Roberts: Our Decision Isn't About Whether Obamacare Is Sound Policy," Talking Points Memo Livewire, June 28, 2012, http://livewire.talkingpointsmemo.com/entries/roberts-our-decision-isnt-about-whether-obamacare-is.

provide protection for immigrants. The statement noted that the US bishops have not sought to overturn the legislation entirely.[171]

Chief Justice Roberts ruled that Obamacare (The Affordable Care Act) was constitutional because "the requirement that every citizen must purchase health insurance—was in effect a tax" and "the Constitution permits such a tax." In other words, he ruled Obamacare constitutional because the Constitution grants Congress the power to levy taxes.

As noted in the same quote from the Catholic World News, the dissenting justices, in a joint opinion, said: "In our view, the act before us is invalid in its entirety."[172] To view the minority opinion in its entirety, see reference at footnote.[173] For more information on the ruling, see "ObamaCare and the Power to Tax" from the Wall Street Journal,[174] "Obamacare: Dissenting Justices Opinion" from the Lorinov's Blog,[175]

---

[171] "Supreme Court Upholds Obama Health-care Reform," Catholic World News, June 28, 2012, http://www.catholicculture.org/news/headlines/index.cfm?storyid=14767.
[172] Ibid.
[173] "SCOTUS Obamacare Ruling: The Dissenting Opinion in it's entirety," Patriots for America, June 28, 2012, http://patriotsforamerica.ning.com/forum/topics/scotus-obamacare-ruling-the-dissenting-opinion-in-it-s-entirety.
[174] ."ObamaCare and the Power to Tax," Wall Street Journal, June 28, 2012, http://online.wsj.com/article/SB10001424052702303561504577495242473319890.html.
[175] Lorinov, "Obamacare: Dissenting Justices Opinion," Lorinov's Blog, June 28, 2012, http://roblorinov.wordpress.com/2012/06/28/obamacare-dissenting-justices-opinion/.

"Obamacare Dissenting Opinion the Original Majority Opinion?" from the Kansas Citian.[176]

CONCLUSION. Was Chief Justice Roberts correct in ruling that Obamacare (The Affordable Care Act) was constitutional because the Constitution grants Congress the power to levy taxes? Absolutely not! He was wrong because the Constitution does not grant Congress the power to force Americans to pay taxes for any purpose not authorized by the Constitution. The Constitution does not even mention healthcare. It does not grant any branch of the federal government authority to levy taxes for healthcare. Congress cannot forcefully take money from one American to pay the healthcare bills of another American.

The minority opinion held that Obamacare (The Affordable Care Act) was "invalid in its entirety." Was the minority opinion correct? Absolutely, because the federal government of the United States is a government of enumerated powers. Each branch of government only has the powers granted to it by the Constitution. Healthcare is not even mentioned in the Constitution. The federal government has absolutely no authority to enact national healthcare. Trying to use the Interstate Commerce Clause or the taxing clauses of the Constitution to justify legislation of national healthcare totally violates the intent of the Founding Fathers to establish a government of limited, enumerated powers and renders the reservation of all other powers to the states quite meaningless.

---

[176] Ed Whelan, "Obamacare Dissenting Opinion the Original Majority Opinion?," Kansas Citian, June 28, 2012, http://thekansascitian.blogspot.com/2012/06/obamacare-dissenting-opinion-original.html.

So what are the consequences of Obamacare for Christians? First, Christians are forced to pay higher federal and state taxes to pay the healthcare bills of other Americans and to fund the killing of millions of unborn or partially born American children. Second, Christians are forced to buy heath insurance or be fined. Third, Christian organizations are forced, against their deeply held moral and religious beliefs, to perform or support abortions, abortive drugs, sterilization, contraceptives, etc. Organizations that fail to comply may be fined and forced into bankruptcy.

CHAPTER 9.6

CLIMATE CHANGE AND ENVIRONMENT

INTRODUCTION. Climate change is one of the very few areas where Democrats are more right than Republicans. However, any American who believes that climate change justifies voting for any Democrat is greatly mistaken. Doing so would be immoral, as revealed in this book.

WINNING VOTES DISHONESTLY. Democrats use arguments about the environment, climate change, and global warming to win votes dishonestly. During elections, they talk about non-polluting renewable energy resources like solar power, wind power, etc. However, use of these energy sources is not economically feasible for most Americans. How many Democrats drive cars powered by solar cells or fuel cells? How is the electricity generated for the few that drive electric cars? Is it generated by a coal plant or nuclear plant? How many Democrats live in a solar or wind heated/cooled home? Most Americans cannot afford to these non-polluting energy sources because they are far too costly. However, Democrats talk about them to win votes.

President Obama promised much greater use of renewable energy resources, but after eight years in office there are absolutely no changes for most Americans. Most Americans will continue to drive gas-powered cars and live in homes heated by gas or electricity from coal or nuclear powered plants. The false claims of Democrats win votes but do nothing to change energy use by Americans.

DOMINION MANDATE. When God created man, He gave the Dominion Mandate: "Be fruitful, and multiply, and replenish the earth, and subdue it: and have dominion over the fish of the sea, and over the fowl of the air, and over every living thing that moveth upon the earth (Gen 1:28, KJV). The Dominion Mandate gives man the duty to care for the earth and use its resources in a responsible manner.

Some Republicans, in the face of overwhelming scientific evidence, deny climate change. I have visited many national parks, and I have seen the evidence of the incredible acceleration in the decline of glaciers. Many shows on the Public Broadcasting Station show scientists researching the results of increasing water temperatures at the poles. Polar bears in Canada and penguins and other wildlife at the poles are losing their ice fields and food supply.

WORSHIP CREATION MORE THAN CREATOR. As a Christian attorney I had to ask myself why Democrats are so very wrong on virtually every topic except climate change. Then I remembered the words of Romans 1.

> For the wrath of God is revealed from heaven against all ungodliness and unrighteousness of men…because that which may be known of God is manifest in them; for God hath shewed it unto them. For the invisible things of him from the creation of the world are clearly seen, being understood by the things that are made, even his eternal power and Godhead; so that they are without excuse: Because that, when they knew God, they glorified him not as God, neither were thankful; but became vain in their imaginations, and their foolish heart was

darkened. Professing themselves to be wise,
they became fools.... Wherefore God also gave
them up.... Who changed the truth of God into
a lie, and <u>worshipped and served the creature
more than the Creator</u>, who is blessed forever.
Amen. Romans 1:18-25 (KJV).

God has revealed Himself to everyone, but some
Democrats have chosen to reject Him and to worship creation
more than the Creator, which is proven by the policies that
they support.

<u>CONCLUSION</u>. Any American who chooses to vote
with Democrats because of concerns about the environment or
climate change is joining forces with them and choosing to
serve "the creature more than the Creator." It is as simple as
that. Also, Americans should not be deceived by dishonest
arguments about using renewable energy sources during
elections. Americans should vote first according to God's laws
and principles revealed through scripture, and second
according to the laws and principles embodied in the
Declaration of Independence, Constitution, and Bill of Rights.

CHAPTER 10.0

CONCLUSION

INTRODUCTION. Trump or Clinton--how would
Christ vote? This chapter answers this question in eight steps.
The first briefly reviews voter guidance from Christian
organizations (Chapter 2). The second addresses voting for the
Supreme Court (Chapter 4). The third discusses scripture
related to Biblical role of government, abortion, and
homosexuality and same-sex marriage (Chapter 5). The fourth
reviews principles embodied in the founding documents i.e.
Declaration of Independence, Constitution, and Bill of Rights
(Chapter 6). The fifth addresses freedoms and rights (Chapter
7). The sixth discusses issues related to truth and character
(Chapter 8). The seventh briefly reviews other issues (Chapter
9). The final section presents concluding remarks.

PRESIDENTIAL VOTER GUIDE. Voting with
Christian voter guidance requires voting Republican. This
begins with the 2016 Presidential Values Voter Presidential
Guide jointly published by Family Research Council and
Family Alliance, the political action arm of Focus on the
Family. Hillary Clinton opposed Christian values on 11 of 12
issues, and her position was unknown on one issue. Trump
supported Christian values on 6 of 12 issues, and his positions
were unknown on 4 issues and mixed on one. He was wrong
on only one position.

CONGRESSIONAL SCORECARDS. Voting with
Congressional Scorecards produced by Christian organizations
requires voting Republican. Democrats score amazingly low
for voting Christian values on (1) the Congressional Scorecard

produced by National Right to Life and (2) the Congressional Scorecard jointly produced by of Family Research Council and Family Alliance. Most Republicans scored 100%. Most Democrats scored 0%. Trump did not serve in Congress, so he was not rated. Clinton, Obama, and Biden all scored zero on both scorecards. They voted against Christian values every time they voted on family-related issues.

SUPREME COURT. Voting for the Supreme Court requires voting Republican. The president appoints Supreme Court justices who serve for life. Republicans and Donald Trump support Supreme Court Justices who uphold the Constitution. Democrats and Hillary Clinton support Supreme Court justices who, contrary to the Constitution, give the federal government authority to grant healthcare, education, and other benefits not mentioned or authorized by the Constitution. See chapters on Supreme Court and Constitution.

BIBLICAL ROLE OF GOVERNMENT. Voting for God's ideal for government requires voting Republican. Democrats believe that God's ideal is government that cares for its citizens. That is why President Obama said, "I believe that I am my brother's keeper!" and why he instituted national healthcare (Obamacare). That is why Hillary Clinton offered generous healthcare and education benefits which never could be afforded by taxpayers. But scripture shows that God's ideal is NOT government that cares for its people. 1 Samuel 8:8-20 shows that God wants his people to look to Him not government for their provision. He warned the Israelites how much a king would take from them (10%). Today national, state, and local governments take far more through many taxes.

The founding fathers understood God's ideal, embodied in the Constitution, of smaller government, lower

218

taxes, and greater personal freedom and responsibility for all citizens. They were fiercely independent men who greatly treasured their freedom and would not trade it for government benefits. The purpose of government is not to provide or care for citizens, but to protect life and liberty and thereby enable the pursuit of happiness. See chapters on Truth About Taxes and Biblical Role of Government.

TAXING THE RICH. Voting for God's ideal on taxes requires voting Republican. What is God's ideal for taxes for the rich and the poor? God's "tax rate" for tithes is exactly the same rate for the rich and the poor: 10% (Lev. 27:30-32). See Deut. 12:5-11; 14:22-28; Num. 18:24-28; Mal. 3:8-10; Heb. 7:1-4. In 1 Sam. 8:8-20, God warned Israel that a king would charge exactly the same for the rich and the poor: 10%. No verse in the 66 books of the Bible even suggests charging higher tax rates for the rich.

Why does God not advocate higher tax rates for the rich? No poor man has any legal or moral right to put a gun to the head of a rich man and demand his money. That is theft. The same principle applies to government. Governments do not have authority to take by force lawfully earned income from one person and give it to another. That is theft by government, and that is what the Democrats strongly advocate in every election. They win votes by promising government benefits not paid for by the poor or "middle class" voting for them, but paid for only by "the rich."

HOMOSEXUALITY AND SAME-SEX MARRIAGE. Voting God's will on homosexuality and same-sex marriage means voting Republican. Scripture teaches that they are extreme perversions of God's design for man, woman, and marriage (Gen. 2:18-24; Lev. 18:22-26; 20:13-16; 1 Tim. 1:9-

10; 1 Cor. 6:9-10; Rom. 1:16-32). Election of Democrats will continue to result in laws that promote homosexuality and same-sex marriage, which are so destructive to families, the most basic, fundamental unit of society and the backbone of our nation.

ABORTION. Voting God's will on abortion means voting Republican. Most Democrats are pro-choice. Most Republicans are pro-life. Scripture shows that in the eyes of God, abortion is murder. See Gen. 16:11; 17:10,12,14; 19:36; 38:24,25; Ex. 21:22-23; 22:22; Lev. 12:2,5; 1 Sam. 4:19; 2 Sam. 11:5; 2Kin. 8:12; 15:16; Isa. 26:17,18; 49:15; 54:1; Jer. 31:8; Hos. 13:16; Am. 1:13; Luke 2:12,16; 18:15-16, Ps. 139:13-16; Job 31:15; Is. 44:2; 44:24: 49:5; Jer. 1:5. See chapter on Abortion.

Most Americans fail to grasp the primary abortion-related issue, which is who pays for abortions. Pro-choice Democrats want to force Americans who consider abortion to be murder to pay for abortions. They only support the choices of those who agree with them. That is the ultimate in hypocrisy. The Constitution does not give the federal government any authority to order any American to pay for abortions of other Americans. It is illegal and unethical for any American to try to force any other American to violate their deeply held moral or religious beliefs by paying for or providing abortions.

Hillary Clinton would continue the pro-abortion policies of President Obama. President Obama used executive orders to divert funds to national and international pro-abortion groups. He refused to cut federal funds (taxpayer dollars) to Planned Parenthood, the nation's number one abortion provider. When several states cut state funds to Planned

Parenthood, President Obama funded it with millions in U.S. taxpayer dollars.

DECLARATION OF INDEPENDENCE. The Declaration of Independence shows that the United States was founded upon belief that: (1) God created all things seen and unseen and all laws that govern all things seen and unseen; (2) God creates all men equal with "certain unalienable Rights…[that include] Life, Liberty and the pursuit of Happiness;" (3) "to secure these rights, Governments are instituted among Men, deriving their just powers from the consent of the governed;" (4) "whenever any…Government becomes destructive of these ends, it is the Right of the People to alter or to abolish it, and to institute new Government;" and (5) this new government must be established in accordance with God's laws to protect these God-given rights.[177]

Voting with and for the Declaration of Independence requires voting Republican. Most Americans who reject the most important principles that the United States was founded upon are Democrats, not Republicans. Most Americans who do not believe in God and creation are Democrats. Most Americans who reject the laws that God created to govern men and governments are Democrats. Any American who votes for any Democrat joins forces with these ungodly fools who reject God and His laws. Also, Republicans better support the rights to life, liberty, the pursuit of happiness, and the right to bear arms. See chapter on Declaration of Independence.

CONSTITUTION. Voting with and for the Constitution requires voting Republican. The primary purpose of the Constitution is to define and limit the powers of each branch of the federal government. The government of the

---

[177] Ibid.

221

United States is a government of enumerated powers. Each branch only has those powers granted to it by the Constitution. All other powers are reserved to the states and to the people. Article I grants powers to Congress (Senate and House of Representatives). Article II grants powers to the executive branch (President). Article III grants powers to the judicial branch (Supreme Court and federal courts). No part of the Constitution grants any branch responsibility or authority for healthcare or education or to care for the poor or the middle class. Democrats reject the limits of power imposed on the federal government by the Constitution. See chapters on Constitution, Truth on Taxes, Democratic Platform, etc.

BILL OF RIGHTS. Voting with and for the Bill of Rights requires voting Republican. The Bill of Rights, the first ten amendments to the Constitution, grants all Americans the rights of freedom of religion, freedom of speech, right to bear arms, right to a criminal defense attorney, etc. The ninth amendment protects other rights of the people. The tenth amendment states that the federal government only has those powers granted to it by the Constitution, and that all other powers are reserved to the states. No part of the Bill of Rights grants any American any right to education, healthcare, or any other social or economic benefits paid for by other Americans.

JURISDICTION OF CHURCH AND STATE. Voting for proper jurisdiction of church and state requires voting Republican. Today most Americans, to include most lawyers and judges, have a totally wrong understanding of the jurisdiction of church and state and the self-evident common sense truths our nation was founded upon. They exclude God, creation, and God's laws from politics, government, schools, and the workplace. They fail to recognize that the United States government was founded upon belief in God and creation, and that all Americans have a duty to properly acknowledge God in politics, government, schools, and the workplace in the same way that our nation's Founding Fathers acknowledged Him and continually asked for his guidance and blessing.

FREEDOM SPEECH AND FREEDOM OF RELIGION. Voting for freedom of speech and freedom of religion requires voting Republican. No group of Americans has more restrictions on its freedom of speech and freedom of religion than Christians. Democrats have tried to silence Christians, to eliminate their competition during elections. A law called the LBJ law, because President Lyndon Baines Johnson pushed it through to silence his critics, threatens a church with loss of tax-exempt status if it endorses a candidate. During 2008, Democrats tried to enact legislation to silence conservative talk shows. Donald Trump promised to reverse the LBJ law.

No President has done more to rob Christians of freedom of religion than President Obama. See chapter on Freedom of Speech and Freedom of Religion for details. If Clinton is elected and Democrats have a majority in the House and Senate, Congress will enact laws to further restrict the freedom of speech and freedom of religion of Christians.

RIGHT TO BEAR ARMS. Voting for the right to bear arms requires voting Republican. The Declaration of Independence and Second Amendment both provide justification for the right to bear arms not for hunting or self-defense, but for defense of good government or overthrow of an abusive government that denies the God-given inalienable rights of life, liberty, and the pursuit of happiness. Thus both the Declaration of Independence and the Second Amendment provide justification for the ownership of military style weapons needed for defense or overthrow of a government.

Nevertheless, Republicans and Democrats should agree on reasonable background checks and reasonable restrictions on who should be denied the right to bear arms. No American who is diagnosed as mentally ill or on a do-not-fly list should be permitted to purchase a weapon without a court hearing to prove the diagnosis or listing as unjustified.

TRUTH ON TAXES. Voting for truth on taxes requires voting Republican. Hillary Clinton, Democrats, and the Democratic Platform tell many of their biggest lies about taxes, and the media never corrects them. They always claim that the "rich" or "wealthy few" are not paying their fair share of taxes and should be taxed more to support the overtaxed "middle class." That is totally false.

All Americans can very quickly verify the truth about taxes by taking a few minutes to go to www.cbo.gov (Congressional Budget Office), click on Taxes or Income Distribution and read the very short article entitled "The Distribution of Household Income and Federal Taxes, 2013" dated June 8, 2016. [178] In 2013, the top 20% of Americans earned 53% of the income and paid 69% of federal taxes. The bottom 20% earned 5% of income and paid only 1% of federal taxes. The middle 20% earned 14% of income and paid only 9% of federal taxes. Another artile in the same area shows that figures for 2011 were almost exactly the same.

---

[178] Go to www.cbo.gov (Congressional Budget Office website), click on Taxes or Income Distribution and read article entitled "The Distribution of Household Income and Federal Taxes, 2013", dated June 8, 2016.

Americans can also go to www.irs.gov and view the 2015 Instructions for Form 1040. Current federal income tax rates range from 10% for the lowest income group to 39.6% for the highest income group (see "2015 Tax Rate Schedules" on page 102). However, actual tax rates are very different due to countless tax deductions and credits that benefit the poor and middle class but are phased out for the wealthy. The end result is that about 49% of Americans, mostly lower and middle class, pay no federal income tax, the rich pay more than their fair share, and the most vilified top 1% pay about 27% of all federal taxes. Democrats will never quote these facts, because they want to win votes with lies and deception. See chapter on Truth on Taxes for more facts about taxes.

LIES AND DECEPTION. Voting against lies and deception means voting Republican. It is absolutely amazing how much politicians use lies and deception to win votes. However, a Republican who uses lies to win votes is a fool who does not realize that the truth is on his side.
Lies are an essential part of the political philosophy and political arguments of Democrats. The entire chapter on False Claims of Politicians presents an amazing alphabetical list of false claims made by Democrats. These include lies about abortion, Constitution, Declaration of Independence, Democratic Platform, education, government (role of), healthcare, homosexuality, right to bear arms, same-sex marriage, separation of church and state, supreme court, taxes, and women's wages.

The Democratic Platform is founded upon lies. If you remove the lies, the Democratic Platform collapses. One of biggest lies is that so many Americans can enjoy so many government benefits without paying for them (healthcare, welfare, education, Social Security, Medicare, abortions, contraceptives, etc.). Democrats buy votes by promising "free" benefits to Americans paid for by other Americans. This gives them great political advantage. It is impossible to pay for all the totally unconstitutional education and healthcare benefits promised by Hillary Clinton and other Democrats by just raising taxes on the rich, who already pay more than their share of taxes. See chapters on Democratic Platform and Taxes.

Why do so many Americans reward dishonest politicians with their support? How is it possible that so many Americans believe all the lies and deception and vote for whoever promises the greatest financial benefit? Why do they not care about what best serves God or the nation? The challenge for Christians is to see through all the lies and false promises and to discern how to vote Christian values.

CHARACTER OF PRESIDENT. Voting for character in our next president requires voting for Donald Trump not Hillary Clinton because the Clintons are guilty of an amazing amount of lies, deception, and political corruption. The chapter on Character in Presidential Candidates shows that lies, deception, and unethical conduct are an integral part of who the Clintons are and what they do. The problem goes far beyond the lies Hillary Clinton about Benghazi, her emails as Secretary of State, and her totally false promises of free college education for most Americans. It goes far beyond all Bill Clinton's sexual indiscretions before and during his presidency.

Americans who want to understand the depth of political corruption of the Clintons should google and watch the free online video "Clinton Cash" or read the book "Clinton Cash: The Untold Story of How and Why Foreign Governments and Businesses Helped Make Bill and Hillary

Rich" by Peter Schweizer.[179] Many millions of dollars were given to Clinton Foundation or paid to the Clintons for speeches in exchange for political favors which greatly profited the Clintons and millionaires and billionaires at the expense of the environment and the poor of other nations. The Associated Press reported that "85 of the 154 people from non-government-related interests who met with or who had scheduled phone calls with Clinton either donated to her family's charitable organization or had committed funds."[180]

All of these "pay to play" deals made the Clintons very wealthy. One deal negotiated by Hillary Clinton gave Russia 20% of United States uranium production, a rare element needed for our own nuclear power plants and nuclear weapons. One deal gave India American nuclear technology. One donor got approval to deforest a rain forest in Bogota and sell the wood to China. In another Hillary reversed her position on the Keystone Excel Pipeline, turning against environmentalists, for money. Deals in Haiti enriched Clinton donors while leaving poor earthquake victims without desperately needed support. See chapter on Character in President for other deals.

Americans who want better understanding of the character of the Clintons may read "Crisis in Character," a book written by former Secret Service Agent Gary J. Byrne, who worked with the Clintons in the White House. Americans may also read the book or see the movie entitled "Hillary's America by Dinesh D'Souza.

---

[179] Peter Schweizer. Clinton Cash: The Untold Story of How and Why Foreign Governments and Businesses Helped Make Bill and Hillary Rich, New York: Harper Publishers, 2015.
[180] Nick Gass, "Clinton mounts full-court press against media," www.politico.com/story/2016/08/clinton-campaign-blasts-massive," downloaded August 24, 2016.

NATIONAL SECURITY. <u>Voting for national security requires voting Republican</u>. Hillary Clinton, like other Democrats, cannot be trusted to make national security or funding of the armed forces of the United States her top priority. Her top priority is taking care of Americans through costly, totally unconstitutional social programs outlined in the Democratic Platform (education, healthcare, etc.).

Also, Hillary Clinton betrayed all Americans by compromising our national security by giving Russia 20% of U.S. uranium production and by giving U.S. nuclear technology to India. Only Donald Trump can be trusted to make national defense his top priority, to restore military strength, and to properly defend Americans from all enemies, foreign and domestic. See chapter on National Security.

JOBS AND ECONOMY. <u>Voting for jobs and the economy means voting for Donald Trump</u>. He is infinitely more qualified to deal with jobs and the economy than Hillary Clinton. Indeed, he may be more educated, more experienced, and more qualified than any other President in the history of the United States. Also, he knows how to build teams to help discharge his responsibilities as President, and he would be much better at negotiating economic, nuclear, military, and other agreements with other nations. See chapter on Jobs and the Economy.

IMMIGRATION. <u>Voting for legal immigration and against illegal immigration requires voting for Donald Trump</u>. Americans who want more protection from immigration of terrorists, illegal drug traffic, and other illegal immigration should vote for Trump. Americans who want fewer restrictions on immigration and the legalization of millions of illegal immigrants should vote for Clinton. Also, Clinton will continue the policies of President Obama, allowing many thousands of immigrants from Syria who cannot be properly vetted. It would be terrorist malpractice for ISIS to fail to infiltrate these immigrants. See chapter on Immigration.

EDUCATION AND HEALTHCARE (OBAMACARE). Voting against totally unconstitutional federal education and healthcare benefits requires voting Republican. No part of Scripture or the Constitution gives the federal government authority to provide education or healthcare benefits to Americans. Congress cannot ethically or legally forcefully take money from one American to pay the education or healthcare bills of another American. See chapters on Education, Healthcare (Obamacare), Constitution, and Bill of Rights.

CLIMATE CHANGE AND ENVIRONMENT. Any American who chooses to vote with Democrats because of concerns about the environment or climate change is choosing to serve "the creature more than the Creator" (see Rom. 1). Americans should not be deceived by dishonest election arguments about using renewable energy sources. After 8 years in office, President Obama has done virtually nothing to change the energy usage of most Americans. See chapter on Climate Change and Environment.

FINAL NOTES. Trump or Clinton—how would Christ vote? This book shows that voting with Christ in 2016 requires voting Republican and voting for Trump for President. It is absolutely amazing how much Democrats are united in voting against Christian values. Democrats strongly align themselves against God and His laws in virtually all areas: freedom of speech, freedom of religion, biblical role of government, taxes, federal spending, federal debt, appointment of judges, abortion, marriage, same-sex marriage, homosexual rights, etc.

Any vote for any Democrat is a vote against scripture, the Declaration of Independence, the Constitution, and the Bill of Rights. No Christian should vote for any Democrat. Christians should not vote for pro-life Democrats. When Democrats control the House or the Senate, they block legislation based on God's laws. When Democrats have a majority in the Senate, they chair the Senate Judiciary Committee and block any pro-life Christian judges from becoming federal judges or Supreme Court Justices. Empowering Democrats enables them to defeat attempts by Christians to return our nation to the Christian principles upon which it was founded.

All Americans answer to God, not man, for everything done to ensure the election of men and women who will govern in accordance with God's laws. Every Christian has a duty to vote for the candidates who will best serve God. Failure to vote for the lesser of evils ensures election of the most evil. Contrary to popular opinion, the most loving thing to do is not to remain silent, be tolerant, avoid divisive issues or avoid being critical or judgmental, but to forcefully and emphatically challenge Christians to love and serve God in greater obedience to the laws and principles that God has revealed through Scripture.

Fear of God is the beginning of wisdom (Pr. 9:10; Ps. 111:10. See Job 28:28; Pr. 1:7; 15:33). Americans should respect and fear God, not man, place their trust in God not man, and vote for men who will govern in obedience to His commandments. Christians should seek better understanding of God's laws, and follow Christ, living and voting in obedience to "the will of [the] Father." They should reach out to others, to lead them from darkness to light, from death to life, and challenge them to live and vote Christian values.

All this is done in vain if it is reluctant, sacrificial obedience to God's will. God is God in all areas of our lives, and we answer to Him for all of our thoughts, words, and actions. However, what God really wants is not reluctant obedience to His commandments but a heart to heart loving relationship with each man, woman, and child. The God who created every atom in every universe has chosen to need our love and devotion. Life apart from God is devoid of meaning. In Him we live and move and have our being.

President John F. Kennedy challenged Americans to a higher calling with the words, "Think not what your country can do for you, but what you can do for your country." A much higher calling is: "Think not what God can do for you, but what you can do for God." The highest calling is the Greatest Commandment: "Thou shalt love the Lord thy God with all thy heart, and with all thy soul, and with all thy mind" (Deut. 6:5; Matt. 22:37-40; Luke 10:27). Every man, woman, and child is called by God to daily put on the full armor of God and to do battle for the Lord and to be salt and light in all areas of life, to include politics, law, and government. Jesus said, "I am come that they might have life, and that they might have it more abundantly" (John 10:11, KJV). This abundant life is only possible if one dies to self and lives for Christ.

BIBLIOGRAPHY

"2012 Democratic Platform, https://www.democrats.org/party-platform (accessed 2/2/2016).

"2015 Tax Rate Schedules," Internal Revenue Service Form 1040 Instructions, p. 102. See also at www.IRS.gov.

"2016 Democratic Platform, https://www.demconvention.com/platform (accessed 8/19/2016).

"2016 Values Voter Presidential Voter Guide." Family Research Council Action, http://www.FRCAction.org (accessed June, 2016).

"Abraham Lincoln Quotes." Thinkexist, http://thinkexist.com /quotes/abraham_lincoln, April 13, 2012.

"Apostles' Creed." Catechism of the Catholic Church. Wikipedia.org., http://en.wikipedia.org/ wiki/Apostles%27_Creed.

Balkin, Karen, Ed. The War on Terrorism: Opposing Viewpoints. New York: Thomson Gale, 2005.

Barton, David. The Bible, Voters & the 2008 Election. Aledo, Texas: Wallbuilder Press, 2008.

Bethany Monk. "Same-Sex Marriage to Become Plank in DNC Platform," Citizenlink, July 31, 2012, http://www.citizenlink.com.

"Bill of Rights." U.S. National Archives & Records Administration, http://www.archives.gov/exhibits/charters/constitution.html.

Black, Henry Campbell. Black's Law Dictionary, 5th Ed., 1979, p 766.

Blakely, Jonathan. "One Top GOP Line of Attack: Kagan's Opposition to Military Recruitment at Harvard Law School's Office of Career Services." ABC News, http://abcnews.go.com/blogs/politics/2010/05/one-top-gop-line-of-attack-kagans-opposition-to-military-recruitment-at-harvard-law-schools-office-of-career-services/.

Bondarchuk's, Sergei. Soviet film adaptation of Leo Tolstoy's book War and Peace.

Bracchi, Paul. "It May Have Been a Victory for Free Speech, But Why Did Breakfast Insult of Muslim's Faith Case Ever Come to Court?", DailyMail, http://www.dailymail.co.uk/news/article-1234680/ It-victory-free-speech-did-breakfast-insult=Muslims-faith-case-come-court.html.

Bruce, Mary. "Obama: Voters Face Starkest Contrast Since Johnson-Goldwater." ABC OTUS News, April 10, 2012.

Burke, Edmund. "Edmund Burke," Wikiquote, http://en.wikiquote.org/wiki/Edmund_Burke.

Byrne, Gary J. Crisis in Character. New York: Center Street Publishers, 2016.

"Can Congress Make Me Buy Health Insurance." Citizenlink, http://www.citizenlink.com/2009/08/24/can-congress-make-me-buy-health-insurance/.

Carpenter, F.B. (1866). "Six Months at the White House," p. 282. Retrieved 2010-02-20. Quoted in "Abraham Lincoln and Religion." TheFreeDictionary, http://encyclopedia.thefreedictionary.com/ Abraham+Lincoln+ and+religion #endnote_rf-17.

Citron, Jamie. "We're Going to be the Edge," October 02, 2008, and "Friends of Barack Visit Ohio," October 06, 2008. LBGT link under "People" at http://pride.barackobama.com.

"Constitution of the United States." U.S. National Archives & Records Administration, http://www.archives.gov/ exhibits/charters/constitution.html.

"Declaration of Independence." U.S. National Archives & Records Administration, http://www.archives.gov/ exhibits/charters/declaration.html.

"The Developing Threat of Freedom of Conscience." Citizenlink, http://www.citizenlink.com/2011/04/15/the-developing-threat-of-freedom-of-conscience/.

D'Souza, Dinesh. America: Imagine a World Without Her. Regnery Publishing, 2014.

D'Souza, Dinesh, John Sullivan, Bruce Schooley. America: Imagine the World Without Her. America Film, LLC, 2014.

D'Souza, Dinesh. Hillary's America: The Secret History of the Democratic Party. Regnery Publishing, 2016.

Edelman, Adam. "Bill Clinton Got $17.6M from Big For-Profit University while Hillary Clinton Vowed 'Crackdown' on their 'Abusive Practices.'" New York Daily News, August 24, 2016.

"Effective Tax Rates." Congressional Budget Office, http://www.cbo.gov/ftpdocs/88xx/doc8885/EffectiveTaxRates.shtml.

Foust, Michael. "Obama: If Elected I Will Use the Bully Pulpit for Gay Causes," Baptist Press, Feb 28, 2008, http://www.bpnews.netbpnews.asp?id=27510 as quoted in October 2008 letter by James Dobson at http://www.citizenlink.com.

"FRC Action: Elena Kagan's Pro-Abortion Record is Far Outside the Mainstream." Family Research Council Action, May 19, 2010, http://www.frcaction.org.

Gass, Nick. "Clinton mounts full-court press against media." http://www.politico.com/story/2016/08/clinton-campaign-blasts-massive," downloaded August 24, 2016.

Hausknecht, Bruce. "Obamacare Decision Next Week: What's at Stake?", June 22, 2012, http://www.citizenlink.com.

Holy Bible, King James Version. Nashville: Thomas Nelson, Inc., 1982.

Holy Bible, New King James Version. Nashville: Thomas Nelson, Inc., 1982.

Holy Bible, New International Version. Grand Rapids: Zondervan Bible Publishing, 1973, 1978, 1984.

Holy Bible, Today's New International Version. Grand Rapids: Zondervan Bible Publishing, 2001, 2005.

Kornblut, Anne E. and Robert Barnes. "Kagan Would Emphasize Supreme Court Moving in New Direction." The Washington Post, May 11, 2010, http://www.washingtonpost.com/wp-dyn/content/article/2010/05/10/AR2010051001116.html.

Lorinov, "Obamacare: Dissenting Justices Opinion," Lorinov's Blog, June 28, 2012, http://roblorinov.wordpress.com/2012/06/28/ obamacare-dissenting-justices-opinion.

Mansfield, Stephen. The Faith of Barack Obama. Nashville, Dallas: Thomas Nelson Publisher, 2008.

"March 2008 Action Update." National Journal, March 7, 2008, http://nj.nationaljournal.com/voteratings. As cited in Focus Action, http://www.citizenlink.org.

Mendell, David. Obama: A Promise of Change. New York: HarperCollins Publishers, 2008.

Monk, Bethany. "HHS Contraception Mandate Deadline Falls Wednesday," Citizenlink, July 31, 2012, http://www.citizenlink.com;

Mulbrandon, Catherine. "How Much Taxes Are Paid by the Poor, Middle Class and Rich," VisualiizingEconomics,

February 2, 2012, http://visualizingeconomics.com/ 2010/02/12/.

Obama, Barack. The Audacity of Hope: Thoughts on Reclaiming the American Dream. New York: Crown Publishers, 2006.

Obama, Barack. "Call to Renewal Keynote Address," June 28, 2006. http://www.Barackobama.com.

Obama, Barack. Change We Can Believe In: Barack Obama's Plan to Renew America's Promise. New York: Three Rivers Press, 2008.

Obama, Barack. Dreams from My Father. New York: Three Rivers Press, 1995.

"Obama Distorts His Abortion Record In Third Debate," National Right to Life Committee, October 16, 2008. http://www.nrlc.org (accessed October 22, 2008).

"ObamaCare and the Power to Tax," Wall Street Journal, June 28, 2012.

"President Obama to Freedom of Religion: Nertz to You!", Family Research Council Action, August 6, 2012, http://www.frcaction.org.

"The Presidential Record on Life: President Barack Obama 2009-present." National Right to Life, http://www.nrlc.org.

"Pro-Life Group Proves That Obama Subsidizes Abortion," Citizenlink, http://www.citizenlink.com/2012/10/29/pro-life-group-proves-that-obamacare-subsidizes-abortion/.

"Report: Rev. Jeremiah Wright Has Affair With Another Man's Wife," Fox News, September 9, 2008. http://FOXNews.com.

Roberts, Chief Justice. "Roberts: Our Decision Isn't About Whether Obamacare Is Sound Policy," Talking Points Memo Livewire, June 28, 2012, http://livewire.talkingpointsmemo.com/entries/roberts-our-decision-isnt-about-whether-obamacare-is.

Roy, Avik. "CBO: Obamacare Will Spend More, Tax More, and Reduce the Deficit Less Than We Previously Thought," Forbes, August 27, 2012, http://www.forbes.com.

Sapet, Karrily. Political Profiles: Barack Obama. Greensboro, North Carolina: Morgan Reynolds Publishing, 2008.

Schweizer, Peter. Clinton Cash: The Untold Story of How and Why Foreign Governments and Businesses Helped Make Bill and Hillary Rich. New York: Harper Publishers, 2015.

"SCOTUS Obamacare Ruling: The Dissenting Opinion in it's entirety," Patriots for America, June 28, 2012, http://patriotsforamerica. ning.com/ forum/topics/ scotus-obamacare-ruling-the-dissenting-opinion-in-it-s-entirety.

"Senator Barack Obama Record on Abortion, United States Senate, Illinois State Senate." National Right to Life Committee, http://www.nrlc.org (accessed August 28, 2008).

"So-Called Hate Speech," Citizenlink, www.citizenlink.com/ 2010/03/citizenlink-so-called-hate-speech/.

"Sotomayor: A Policy Maker or a Jurist?", Family Research Council Action, May 26, 2009, http://www.frcaction.org.

Stanek, Jill. "Obama Blocked Born Alive Infant Protection Act," April 2, 2008. National Right to Life Committee. http://www.nrlc.org (accessed July 7, 2008).

Steele, Shelby. A Bound Man: Why We Are Excited about Barack Obama and Why He Can't Win. New York: Free Press, 2008.

Street, Paul. Barack Obama and the Future of American Politics. Boulder, Colorado: Paradigm Publishers, 2008.

"Supreme Court Upholds Obama Health-care Reform." Catholic World News, June 28, 2012, http://www.catholicculture.org/ news/headlines/ index.cfm?storyid=14767.

"Supreme Court's Obamacare Decision: Full Text." The Atlantic, June 28, 2012, http://www.theatlantic.com/politics/archive/2012/06/the-supreme-courts-obamacare-decision-full-text/259102/.

Thompson, Derek. "The Health Care Decision Explained in 1 Paragraph on SCOTUSblog," The Atlantic, June 28, 2012, http://www.theatlantic.com/business/archive/2012/06/the-health-care-decision-explained-in-1-paragraph-on-scotusblog/259097/

Titus, Herbert W. God, Man, and Law: The Biblical Principles. Oak Brook, Illinois: Institute in Basic Life Principles, 1994.

Tobias, Carol. "Statement by Carol Tobias, National Right to Life President," April 12, 2012, State Senate, http://www.nrlc.org.

"UK Pastor Arrested Over Comments on Homosexuality," Citizenlink, http://www.citizenlink.com/2010/05/citizenlink-uk-pastor-arrested-over-comments-on-homosexuality/.

"Values Voter Guide for 2008 Presidential Candidates." Family Research Council Action, http://www.frcaction.org (accessed July 9, 2008).

Van Der Vat, Dan. Pearl Harbor: The Day of Infamy—An Illustrated History. New York: Basic Books, 2001. Introduction by Senator John McCain.

"Vote Scorecard." Family Research Council Action, http://www.frcaction.org (accessed July 9, 2008).

"Vote Scorecard." Family Research Council Action, http://www.frcaction.org (accessed February 17, 2012).

"Vote Scorecard." Focus on the Family Action, http://www.citizenlink.org (accessed July 9, 2008).

"Vote Scorecard." National Right to Life Committee, http://www.nrlc.org (accessed July 7, 2008).

"Vote Scorecard." National Right to Life Committee, http://www.nrlc.org (accessed February 17, 2012).

Wagner, Heather. Barack Obama. New York: Chelsea House Publishers, 2008.

Whelan, Ed. "Obamacare Dissenting Opinion the Original Majority Opinion?," Kansas Citian, June 28, 2012, http://thekansascitian.blogspot.com/2012/06/obamacare-dissenting-opinion-original.html

"Where Do the Candidates Stand on Life: John McCain, Barack Obama," National Right to Life Committee, http://www.nrlc.org (accessed August 28, 2008).

"Where Do the Candidates Stand on Life: Mitt Romney, Barack Obama," National Right to Life Committee. http://www.nrlc.org.

"Why Did Hillary Clinton Need a Private Server? The Answer Makes Bernie Sanders President," www.TheHuffingtonPost.com, downloaded March 7, 2016.

"Widdecombe and Gay Tory Defend Cornish BB Owners, The Christian Institute, http://www.christian.org.uk/news/widdecombe-and-gay-tory-defend-cornish-bb-owners/.

APPENDIX A

DECLARATION OF INDEPENDENCE[181]

IN CONGRESS, July 4, 1776.

The unanimous Declaration of the thirteen united States of America,
When in the Course of human events, it becomes necessary for one people
to dissolve the political bands which have connected them with another,
and to assume among the powers of the earth, the separate and equal station
to which the Laws of Nature and of Nature's God entitle them, a decent
respect to the opinions of mankind requires that they should declare the
causes which impel them to the separation.

We hold these truths to be self-evident, that all men are created equal, that
they are endowed by their Creator with certain unalienable Rights, that
among these are Life, Liberty and the pursuit of Happiness.--That to secure
these rights, Governments are instituted among Men, deriving their just
powers from the consent of the governed, --That whenever any Form of
Government becomes destructive of these ends, it is the Right of the People
to alter or to abolish it, and to institute new Government, laying its
foundation on such principles and organizing its powers in such form, as to
them shall seem most likely to effect their Safety and Happiness. Prudence,
indeed, will dictate that Governments long established should not be
changed for light and transient causes; and accordingly all experience hath
shewn, that mankind are more disposed to suffer, while evils are sufferable,
than to right themselves by abolishing the forms to which they are
accustomed. But when a long train of abuses and usurpations, pursuing
invariably the same Object evinces a design to reduce them under absolute
Despotism, it is their right, it is their duty, to throw off such Government,
and to provide new Guards for their future security.--Such has been the
patient sufferance of these Colonies; and such is now the necessity which
constrains them to alter their former Systems of Government. The history
of the present King of Great Britain is a history of repeated injuries and
usurpations, all having in direct object the establishment of an absolute

---

[181] U.S. National Archives & Records Administration, "The Charters of
Freedom: The Declaration of Independence,"
http://www.archives.gov/exhibits/charters.

Tyranny over these States. To prove this, let Facts be submitted to a candid world.

He has refused his Assent to Laws, the most wholesome and necessary for the public good.

He has forbidden his Governors to pass Laws of immediate and pressing importance, unless suspended in their operation till his Assent should be obtained; and when so suspended, he has utterly neglected to attend to them.

He has refused to pass other Laws for the accommodation of large districts of people, unless those people would relinquish the right of Representation in the Legislature, a right inestimable to them and formidable to tyrants only.

He has called together legislative bodies at places unusual, uncomfortable, and distant from the depository of their public Records, for the sole purpose of fatiguing them into compliance with his measures.

He has dissolved Representative Houses repeatedly, for opposing with manly firmness his invasions on the rights of the people.

He has refused for a long time, after such dissolutions, to cause others to be elected; whereby the Legislative powers, incapable of Annihilation, have returned to the People at large for their exercise; the State remaining in the mean time exposed to all the dangers of invasion from without, and convulsions within.

He has endeavoured to prevent the population of these States; for that purpose obstructing the Laws for Naturalization of Foreigners; refusing to pass others to encourage their migrations hither, and raising the conditions of new Appropriations of Lands.

He has obstructed the Administration of Justice, by refusing his Assent to Laws for establishing Judiciary powers.

He has made Judges dependent on his Will alone, for the tenure of their offices, and the amount and payment of their salaries.

He has erected a multitude of New Offices, and sent hither swarms of Officers to harrass our people, and eat out their substance.

He has kept among us, in times of peace, Standing Armies without the Consent of our legislatures.

He has affected to render the Military independent of and superior to the Civil power.

He has combined with others to subject us to a jurisdiction foreign to our constitution, and unacknowledged by our laws; giving his Assent to their Acts of pretended Legislation:

For Quartering large bodies of armed troops among us:
For protecting them, by a mock Trial, from punishment for any
Murders which they should commit on the Inhabitants of these
States:
For cutting off our Trade with all parts of the world:
For imposing Taxes on us without our Consent:
For depriving us in many cases, of the benefits of Trial by Jury:
For transporting us beyond Seas to be tried for pretended offences
For abolishing the free System of English Laws in a neighbouring
Province, establishing therein an Arbitrary government, and
enlarging its Boundaries so as to render it at once an example and
fit instrument for introducing the same absolute rule into these
Colonies:
For taking away our Charters, abolishing our most valuable Laws,
and altering fundamentally the Forms of our Governments:
For suspending our own Legislatures, and declaring themselves
invested with power to legislate for us in all cases whatsoever.
He has abdicated Government here, by declaring us out of his
Protection and waging War against us.
He has plundered our seas, ravaged our Coasts, burnt our towns,
and destroyed the lives of our people.
He is at this time transporting large Armies of foreign Mercenaries
to compleat the works of death, desolation and tyranny, already
begun with circumstances of Cruelty & perfidy scarcely paralleled
in the most barbarous ages, and totally unworthy the Head of a
civilized nation.
He has constrained our fellow Citizens taken Captive on the high
Seas to bear Arms against their Country, to become the
executioners of their friends and Brethren, or to fall themselves by
their Hands.
He has excited domestic insurrections amongst us, and has
endeavoured to bring on the inhabitants of our frontiers, the
merciless Indian Savages, whose known rule of warfare, is an
undistinguished destruction of all ages, sexes and conditions.

In every stage of these Oppressions We have Petitioned for Redress in the
most humble terms: Our repeated Petitions have been answered only by
repeated injury. A Prince whose character is thus marked by every act
which may define a Tyrant, is unfit to be the ruler of a free people.
Nor have We been wanting in attentions to our Brittish brethren. We have
warned them from time to time of attempts by their legislature to extend an

unwarrantable jurisdiction over us. We have reminded them of the circumstances of our emigration and settlement here. We have appealed to their native justice and magnanimity, and we have conjured them by the ties of our common kindred to disavow these usurpations, which, would inevitably interrupt our connections and correspondence. They too have been deaf to the voice of justice and of consanguinity. We must, therefore, acquiesce in the necessity, which denounces our Separation, and hold them, as we hold the rest of mankind, Enemies in War, in Peace Friends.

We, therefore, the Representatives of the united States of America, in General Congress, Assembled, appealing to the Supreme Judge of the world for the rectitude of our intentions, do, in the Name, and by Authority of the good People of these Colonies, solemnly publish and declare, That these United Colonies are, and of Right ought to be Free and Independent States; that they are Absolved from all Allegiance to the British Crown, and that all political connection between them and the State of Great Britain, is and ought to be totally dissolved; and that as Free and Independent States, they have full Power to levy War, conclude Peace, contract Alliances, establish Commerce, and to do all other Acts and Things which Independent States may of right do. And for the support of this Declaration, with a firm reliance on the protection of divine Providence, we mutually pledge to each other our Lives, our Fortunes and our sacred Honor.

The 56 signatures on the Declaration appear in the positions indicated:

Column 1

Georgia:

Button Gwinnett

Lyman Hall

George Walton

Column 2

North Carolina:

William Hooper

Joseph Hewes

John Penn

South Carolina:

Edward Rutledge

Thomas Heyward, Jr.

Thomas Lynch, Jr.

Arthur Middleton

Column 3

Massachusetts:

John Hancock

Maryland:

Samuel Chase

William Paca

Thomas Stone

Charles Carroll of Carrollton

Virginia:

George Wythe

Richard Henry Lee

Thomas Jefferson

Benjamin Harrison

Thomas Nelson, Jr.

Francis Lightfoot Lee

Carter Braxton

Column 4

Pennsylvania:

Robert Morris

Benjamin Rush

Benjamin Franklin

John Morton

George Clymer

James Smith

George Taylor

James Wilson

George Ross

Delaware:

Caesar Rodney

George Read

Thomas McKean

Column 5

New York:

William Floyd

Philip Livingston

Francis Lewis

Lewis Morris

New Jersey:

Richard Stockton

APPENDIX B

CONSTITUTION OF THE UNITED STATES[182]

Note: The following text is a transcription of the Constitution in its original form. Items that are [underlined] hyperlinked have since been amended or superseded.

We the People of the United States, in Order to form a more perfect Union, establish Justice, insure domestic Tranquility, provide for the common defence, promote the general Welfare, and secure the Blessings of Liberty to ourselves and our Posterity, do ordain and establish this Constitution for the United States of America.

Article. I.
Section. 1.
All legislative Powers herein granted shall be vested in a Congress of the United States, which shall consist of a Senate and House of Representatives.

Section. 2.
The House of Representatives shall be composed of Members chosen every second Year by the People of the several States, and the Electors in each State shall have the Qualifications requisite for Electors of the most numerous Branch of the State Legislature.

No Person shall be a Representative who shall not have attained to the Age of twenty five Years, and been seven Years a Citizen of the United States, and who shall not, when elected, be an Inhabitant of that State in which he shall be chosen.

Representatives and direct Taxes shall be apportioned among the several States which may be included within this Union, according to their respective Numbers, which shall be determined by adding to the whole Number of free

---

[182] U.S. National Archives and Records Administration. "The Charters of Freedom: The Constitution of the United States," http://www.archives.gov/exhibits/charters.

Persons, including those bound to Service for a Term of Years, and excluding Indians not taxed, three fifths of all other Persons. The actual Enumeration shall be made within three Years after the first Meeting of the Congress of the United States, and within every subsequent Term of ten Years, in such Manner as they shall by Law direct. The Number of Representatives shall not exceed one for every thirty Thousand, but each State shall have at Least one Representative; and until such enumeration shall be made, the State of New Hampshire shall be entitled to chuse three, Massachusetts eight, Rhode-Island and Providence Plantations one, Connecticut five, New-York six, New Jersey four, Pennsylvania eight, Delaware one, Maryland six, Virginia ten, North Carolina five, South Carolina five, and Georgia three.

When vacancies happen in the Representation from any State, the Executive Authority thereof shall issue Writs of Election to fill such Vacancies.

The House of Representatives shall chuse their Speaker and other Officers; and shall have the sole Power of Impeachment.

Section. 3.

The Senate of the United States shall be composed of two Senators from each State, chosen by the Legislature thereof for six Years; and each Senator shall have one Vote.

Immediately after they shall be assembled in Consequence of the first Election, they shall be divided as equally as may be into three Classes. The Seats of the Senators of the first Class shall be vacated at the Expiration of the second Year, of the second Class at the Expiration of the fourth Year, and of the third Class at the Expiration of the sixth Year, so that one third may be chosen every second Year; and if Vacancies happen by Resignation, or otherwise, during the Recess of the Legislature of any State, the Executive thereof may make temporary Appointments until the next Meeting of the Legislature, which shall then fill such Vacancies.

No Person shall be a Senator who shall not have attained to the Age of thirty Years, and been nine Years a Citizen of the United States, and who shall not, when elected, be an Inhabitant of that State for which he shall be chosen.

The Vice President of the United States shall be President of the Senate, but shall have no Vote, unless they be equally divided.

The Senate shall chuse their other Officers, and also a President pro tempore, in the Absence of the Vice President, or when he shall exercise the Office of President of the United States.

The Senate shall have the sole Power to try all Impeachments. When sitting for that Purpose, they shall be on Oath or Affirmation. When the President of the United States is tried, the Chief Justice shall preside: And no Person shall be convicted without the Concurrence of two thirds of the Members present.

Judgment in Cases of Impeachment shall not extend further than to removal from Office, and disqualification to hold and enjoy any Office of honor, Trust or Profit under the United States: but the Party convicted shall nevertheless be liable and subject to Indictment, Trial, Judgment and Punishment, according to Law.

Section. 4.
The Times, Places and Manner of holding Elections for Senators and Representatives, shall be prescribed in each State by the Legislature thereof; but the Congress may at any time by Law make or alter such Regulations, except as to the Places of chusing Senators.
The Congress shall assemble at least once in every Year, and such Meeting shall be on the first Monday in December, unless they shall by Law appoint a different Day.

Section. 5.
Each House shall be the Judge of the Elections, Returns and Qualifications of its own Members, and a Majority of each shall constitute a Quorum to do Business; but a smaller Number may adjourn from day to day, and may be authorized to compel the Attendance of absent Members, in such Manner, and under such Penalties as each House may provide.
Each House may determine the Rules of its Proceedings, punish its Members for disorderly Behaviour, and, with the Concurrence of two thirds, expel a Member.
Each House shall keep a Journal of its Proceedings, and from time to time publish the same, excepting such Parts as may in their Judgment require Secrecy; and the Yeas and Nays of the Members of either House on any question shall, at the Desire of one fifth of those Present, be entered on the Journal.
Neither House, during the Session of Congress, shall, without the Consent of the other, adjourn for more than three days, nor to any other Place than that in which the two Houses shall be sitting.

Section. 6.
The Senators and Representatives shall receive a Compensation for their Services, to be ascertained by Law, and paid out of the Treasury of the United States. They shall in all Cases, except Treason, Felony and Breach of the Peace, be privileged from Arrest during their Attendance at the Session of their respective Houses, and in going to and returning from the same; and for any Speech or Debate in either House, they shall not be questioned in any other Place.

No Senator or Representative shall, during the Time for which he was elected, be appointed to any civil Office under the Authority of the United States, which shall have been created, or the Emoluments whereof shall have been encreased during such time; and no Person holding any Office under the United States, shall be a Member of either House during his Continuance in Office.

Section. 7.

All Bills for raising Revenue shall originate in the House of Representatives; but the Senate may propose or concur with Amendments as on other Bills. Every Bill which shall have passed the House of Representatives and the Senate, shall, before it become a Law, be presented to the President of the United States: If he approve he shall sign it, but if not he shall return it, with his Objections to that House in which it shall have originated, who shall enter the Objections at large on their Journal, and proceed to reconsider it. If after such Reconsideration two thirds of that House shall agree to pass the Bill, it shall be sent, together with the Objections, to the other House, by which it shall likewise be reconsidered, and if approved by two thirds of that House, it shall become a Law. But in all such Cases the Votes of both Houses shall be determined by yeas and Nays, and the Names of the Persons voting for and against the Bill shall be entered on the Journal of each House respectively. If any Bill shall not be returned by the President within ten Days (Sundays excepted) after it shall have been presented to him, the Same shall be a Law, in like Manner as if he had signed it, unless the Congress by their Adjournment prevent its Return, in which Case it shall not be a Law.

Every Order, Resolution, or Vote to which the Concurrence of the Senate and House of Representatives may be necessary (except on a question of Adjournment) shall be presented to the President of the United States; and before the Same shall take Effect, shall be approved by him, or being disapproved by him, shall be repassed by two thirds of the Senate and House of Representatives, according to the Rules and Limitations prescribed in the Case of a Bill.

Section. 8.

The Congress shall have Power To lay and collect Taxes, Duties, Imposts and Excises, to pay the Debts and provide for the common Defence and general Welfare of the United States; but all Duties, Imposts and Excises shall be uniform throughout the United States;
To borrow Money on the credit of the United States;
To regulate Commerce with foreign Nations, and among the several States, and with the Indian Tribes;

To establish an uniform Rule of Naturalization, and uniform Laws on the subject of Bankruptcies throughout the United States;

To coin Money, regulate the Value thereof, and of foreign Coin, and fix the Standard of Weights and Measures;

To provide for the Punishment of counterfeiting the Securities and current Coin of the United States;

To establish Post Offices and post Roads;

To promote the Progress of Science and useful Arts, by securing for limited Times to Authors and Inventors the exclusive Right to their respective Writings and Discoveries;

To constitute Tribunals inferior to the supreme Court;

To define and punish Piracies and Felonies committed on the high Seas, and Offences against the Law of Nations;

To declare War, grant Letters of Marque and Reprisal, and make Rules concerning Captures on Land and Water;

To raise and support Armies, but no Appropriation of Money to that Use shall be for a longer Term than two Years;

To provide and maintain a Navy;

To make Rules for the Government and Regulation of the land and naval Forces;

To provide for calling forth the Militia to execute the Laws of the Union, suppress Insurrections and repel Invasions;

To provide for organizing, arming, and disciplining, the Militia, and for governing such Part of them as may be employed in the Service of the United States, reserving to the States respectively, the Appointment of the Officers, and the Authority of training the Militia according to the discipline prescribed by Congress;

To exercise exclusive Legislation in all Cases whatsoever, over such District (not exceeding ten Miles square) as may, by Cession of particular States, and the Acceptance of Congress, become the Seat of the Government of the United States, and to exercise like Authority over all Places purchased by the Consent of the Legislature of the State in which the Same shall be, for the Erection of Forts, Magazines, Arsenals, dock-Yards, and other needful Buildings;--And

To make all Laws which shall be necessary and proper for carrying into Execution the foregoing Powers, and all other Powers vested by this Constitution in the Government of the United States, or in any Department or Officer thereof.

Section. 9.

The Migration or Importation of such Persons as any of the States now existing shall think proper to admit, shall not be prohibited by the Congress prior to the Year one thousand eight hundred and eight, but a Tax or duty may be imposed on such Importation, not exceeding ten dollars for each Person.

The Privilege of the Writ of Habeas Corpus shall not be suspended, unless when in Cases of Rebellion or Invasion the public Safety may require it.

No Bill of Attainder or ex post facto Law shall be passed.

No Capitation, or other direct, Tax shall be laid, <u>unless in Proportion to the Census or enumeration herein before directed to be taken</u>.

No Tax or Duty shall be laid on Articles exported from any State.

No Preference shall be given by any Regulation of Commerce or Revenue to the Ports of one State over those of another; nor shall Vessels bound to, or from, one State, be obliged to enter, clear, or pay Duties in another.

No Money shall be drawn from the Treasury, but in Consequence of Appropriations made by Law; and a regular Statement and Account of the Receipts and Expenditures of all public Money shall be published from time to time.

No Title of Nobility shall be granted by the United States: And no Person holding any Office of Profit or Trust under them, shall, without the Consent of the Congress, accept of any present, Emolument, Office, or Title, of any kind whatever, from any King, Prince, or foreign State.

Section. 10.

No State shall enter into any Treaty, Alliance, or Confederation; grant Letters of Marque and Reprisal; coin Money; emit Bills of Credit; make any Thing but gold and silver Coin a Tender in Payment of Debts; pass any Bill of Attainder, ex post facto Law, or Law impairing the Obligation of Contracts, or grant any Title of Nobility.

No State shall, without the Consent of the Congress, lay any Imposts or Duties on Imports or Exports, except what may be absolutely necessary for executing it's inspection Laws: and the net Produce of all Duties and Imposts, laid by any State on Imports or Exports, shall be for the Use of the Treasury of the United States; and all such Laws shall be subject to the Revision and Controul of the Congress.

No State shall, without the Consent of Congress, lay any Duty of Tonnage, keep Troops, or Ships of War in time of Peace, enter into any Agreement or Compact with another State, or with a foreign Power, or engage in War, unless actually invaded, or in such imminent Danger as will not admit of delay.

Article. II.

Section. 1.

The executive Power shall be vested in a President of the United States of America. He shall hold his Office during the Term of four Years, and, together with the Vice President, chosen for the same Term, be elected, as follows:

Each State shall appoint, in such Manner as the Legislature thereof may direct, a Number of Electors, equal to the whole Number of Senators and Representatives to which the State may be entitled in the Congress: but no Senator or Representative, or Person holding an Office of Trust or Profit under the United States, shall be appointed an Elector.

The Electors shall meet in their respective States, and vote by Ballot for two Persons, of whom one at least shall not be an Inhabitant of the same State with themselves. And they shall make a List of all the Persons voted for, and of the Number of Votes for each; which List they shall sign and certify, and transmit sealed to the Seat of the Government of the United States, directed to the President of the Senate. The President of the Senate shall, in the Presence of the Senate and House of Representatives, open all the Certificates, and the Votes shall then be counted. The Person having the greatest Number of Votes shall be the President, if such Number be a Majority of the whole Number of Electors appointed; and if there be more than one who have such Majority, and have an equal Number of Votes, then the House of Representatives shall immediately chuse by Ballot one of them for President; and if no Person have a Majority, then from the five highest on the List the said House shall in like Manner chuse the President. But in chusing the President, the Votes shall be taken by States, the Representation from each State having one Vote; A quorum for this purpose shall consist of a Member or Members from two thirds of the States, and a Majority of all the States shall be necessary to a Choice. In every Case, after the Choice of the President, the Person having the greatest Number of Votes of the Electors shall be the Vice President. But if there should remain two or more who have equal Votes, the Senate shall chuse from them by Ballot the Vice President.

The Congress may determine the Time of chusing the Electors, and the Day on which they shall give their Votes; which Day shall be the same throughout the United States.

No Person except a natural born Citizen, or a Citizen of the United States, at the time of the Adoption of this Constitution, shall be eligible to the Office of President; neither shall any Person be eligible to that Office who shall not have attained to the Age of thirty five Years, and been fourteen Years a Resident within the United States.

In Case of the Removal of the President from Office, or of his Death, Resignation, or Inability to discharge the Powers and Duties of the said Office, the Same shall devolve on the Vice President, and the Congress may by Law provide for the Case of Removal, Death, Resignation or Inability, both of the President and Vice President, declaring what Officer shall then act as President, and such Officer shall act accordingly, until the Disability be removed, or a President shall be elected.

The President shall, at stated Times, receive for his Services, a Compensation, which shall neither be increased nor diminished during the Period for which he shall have been elected, and he shall not receive within that Period any other Emolument from the United States, or any of them.

Before he enter on the Execution of his Office, he shall take the following Oath or Affirmation:--"I do solemnly swear (or affirm) that I will faithfully execute the Office of President of the United States, and will to the best of my Ability, preserve, protect and defend the Constitution of the United States."

Section. 2.

The President shall be Commander in Chief of the Army and Navy of the United States, and of the Militia of the several States, when called into the actual Service of the United States; he may require the Opinion, in writing, of the principal Officer in each of the executive Departments, upon any Subject relating to the Duties of their respective Offices, and he shall have Power to grant Reprieves and Pardons for Offences against the United States, except in Cases of Impeachment.

He shall have Power, by and with the Advice and Consent of the Senate, to make Treaties, provided two thirds of the Senators present concur; and he shall nominate, and by and with the Advice and Consent of the Senate, shall appoint Ambassadors, other public Ministers and Consuls, Judges of the supreme Court, and all other Officers of the United States, whose Appointments are not herein otherwise provided for, and which shall be established by Law: but the Congress may by Law vest the Appointment of such inferior Officers, as they think proper, in the President alone, in the Courts of Law, or in the Heads of Departments.

The President shall have Power to fill up all Vacancies that may happen during the Recess of the Senate, by granting Commissions which shall expire at the End of their next Session.

Section. 3.

He shall from time to time give to the Congress Information of the State of the Union, and recommend to their Consideration such Measures as he shall judge necessary and expedient; he may, on extraordinary Occasions, convene both Houses, or either of them, and in Case of Disagreement between them, with Respect to the Time of Adjournment, he may adjourn them to such Time as he shall think proper; **he shall receive Ambassadors and other public Ministers; he shall take Care that the Laws be faithfully executed**, and shall Commission all the Officers of the United States.

Section. 4.
The President, Vice President and all civil Officers of the United States, shall be removed from Office on Impeachment for, and Conviction of, Treason, Bribery, or other high Crimes and Misdemeanors.

Article III.
Section. 1.
The judicial Power of the United States shall be vested in one supreme Court, and in such inferior Courts as the Congress may from time to time ordain and establish. The Judges, both of the supreme and inferior Courts, shall hold their Offices during good Behaviour, and shall, at stated Times, receive for their Services a Compensation, which shall not be diminished during their Continuance in Office.

Section. 2.
The judicial Power shall extend to all Cases, in Law and Equity, arising under this Constitution, the Laws of the United States, and Treaties made, or which shall be made, under their Authority;--to all Cases affecting Ambassadors, other public Ministers and Consuls;--to all Cases of admiralty and maritime Jurisdiction;--to Controversies to which the United States shall be a Party;--to Controversies between two or more States;-- between a State and Citizens of another State;--between Citizens of different States;--between Citizens of the same State claiming Lands under Grants of different States, and between a State, or the Citizens thereof, and foreign States, Citizens or Subjects.
In all Cases affecting Ambassadors, other public Ministers and Consuls, and those in which a State shall be Party, the supreme Court shall have original Jurisdiction. In all the other Cases before mentioned, the supreme Court shall have appellate Jurisdiction, both as to Law and Fact, with such Exceptions, and under such Regulations as the Congress shall make.
The Trial of all Crimes, except in Cases of Impeachment, shall be by Jury; and such Trial shall be held in the State where the said Crimes shall have been committed; but when not committed within any State, the Trial shall be at such Place or Places as the Congress may by Law have directed.

Section. 3.

Treason against the United States, shall consist only in levying War against them, or in adhering to their Enemies, giving them Aid and Comfort. No Person shall be convicted of Treason unless on the Testimony of two Witnesses to the same overt Act, or on Confession in open Court.

The Congress shall have Power to declare the Punishment of Treason, but no Attainder of Treason shall work Corruption of Blood, or Forfeiture except during the Life of the Person attainted.

Article. IV.

Section. 1.

Full Faith and Credit shall be given in each State to the public Acts, Records, and judicial Proceedings of every other State. And the Congress may by general Laws prescribe the Manner in which such Acts, Records and Proceedings shall be proved, and the Effect thereof.

Section. 2.

The Citizens of each State shall be entitled to all Privileges and Immunities of Citizens in the several States.

A Person charged in any State with Treason, Felony, or other Crime, who shall flee from Justice, and be found in another State, shall on Demand of the executive Authority of the State from which he fled, be delivered up, to be removed to the State having Jurisdiction of the Crime.

No Person held to Service or Labour in one State, under the Laws thereof, escaping into another, shall, in Consequence of any Law or Regulation therein, be discharged from such Service or Labour, but shall be delivered up on Claim of the Party to whom such Service or Labour may be due.

Section. 3.

New States may be admitted by the Congress into this Union; but no new State shall be formed or erected within the Jurisdiction of any other State; nor any State be formed by the Junction of two or more States, or Parts of States, without the Consent of the Legislatures of the States concerned as well as of the Congress.

The Congress shall have Power to dispose of and make all needful Rules and Regulations respecting the Territory or other Property belonging to the United States; and nothing in this Constitution shall be so construed as to Prejudice any Claims of the United States, or of any particular State.

Section. 4.

The United States shall guarantee to every State in this Union a Republican Form of Government, and shall protect each of them against Invasion; and on

Application of the Legislature, or of the Executive (when the Legislature cannot be convened), against domestic Violence.

Article. V.

The Congress, whenever two thirds of both Houses shall deem it necessary, shall propose Amendments to this Constitution, or, on the Application of the Legislatures of two thirds of the several States, shall call a Convention for proposing Amendments, which, in either Case, shall be valid to all Intents and Purposes, as Part of this Constitution, when ratified by the Legislatures of three fourths of the several States, or by Conventions in three fourths thereof, as the one or the other Mode of Ratification may be proposed by the Congress; Provided that no Amendment which may be made prior to the Year One thousand eight hundred and eight shall in any Manner affect the first and fourth Clauses in the Ninth Section of the first Article; and that no State, without its Consent, shall be deprived of its equal Suffrage in the Senate.

Article. VI.

All Debts contracted and Engagements entered into, before the Adoption of this Constitution, shall be as valid against the United States under this Constitution, as under the Confederation.

This Constitution, and the Laws of the United States which shall be made in Pursuance thereof; and all Treaties made, or which shall be made, under the Authority of the United States, shall be the supreme Law of the Land; and the Judges in every State shall be bound thereby, any Thing in the Constitution or Laws of any State to the Contrary notwithstanding.

The Senators and Representatives before mentioned, and the Members of the several State Legislatures, and all executive and judicial Officers, both of the United States and of the several States, shall be bound by Oath or Affirmation, to support this Constitution; but no religious Test shall ever be required as a Qualification to any Office or public Trust under the United States.

Article. VII.

The Ratification of the Conventions of nine States, shall be sufficient for the Establishment of this Constitution between the States so ratifying the Same.

The Word, "the," being interlined between the seventh and eighth Lines of the first Page, the Word "Thirty" being partly written on an Erazure in the fifteenth Line of the first Page, The Words "is tried" being interlined between the thirty second and thirty third Lines of the first Page and the Word "the" being interlined between the forty third and forty fourth Lines of the second Page.

Attest William Jackson Secretary

Done in Convention by the Unanimous Consent of the States present the Seventeenth Day of September in the Year of our Lord one thousand seven hundred and Eighty seven and of the Independence of the United States of America the Twelfth In witness whereof We have hereunto subscribed our Names,

G°. Washington
Presidt and deputy from Virginia
Delaware
Geo: Read
Gunning Bedford jun
John Dickinson
Richard Bassett
Jaco: Broom
Maryland
James McHenry
Dan of St Thos. Jenifer
Danl. Carroll
Virginia
John Blair
James Madison Jr.
North Carolina
Wm. Blount
Richd. Dobbs Spaight
Hu Williamson
South Carolina
J. Rutledge
Charles Cotesworth Pinckney
Charles Pinckney
Pierce Butler
Georgia
William Few
Abr Baldwin
New Hampshire
John Langdon
Nicholas Gilman

Massachusetts
Nathaniel Gorham
Rufus King
Connecticut
Wm. Saml. Johnson
Roger Sherman
New York
Alexander Hamilton
New Jersey
Wil: Livingston
David Brearley
Wm. Paterson
Jona: Dayton
Pennsylvania
B Franklin
Thomas Mifflin
Robt. Morris
Geo. Clymer
Thos. FitzSimons
Jared Ingersoll
James Wilson
Gouv Morris

APPENDIX C

BILL OF RIGHTS[183]

The Preamble to The Bill of Rights **Congress of the United States** begun and held at the City of New-York, on Wednesday the fourth of March, one thousand seven hundred and eighty nine.

THE Conventions of a number of the States, having at the time of their adopting the Constitution, expressed a desire, in order to prevent misconstruction or abuse of its powers, that further declaratory and restrictive clauses should be added: And as extending the ground of public confidence in the Government, will best ensure the beneficent ends of its institution.

RESOLVED by the Senate and House of Representatives of the United States of America, in Congress assembled, two thirds of both Houses concurring, that the following Articles be proposed to the Legislatures of the several States, as amendments to the Constitution of the United States, all, or any of which Articles, when ratified by three fourths of the said Legislatures, to be valid to all intents and purposes, as part of the said Constitution; viz.

ARTICLES in addition to, and Amendment of the Constitution of the United States of America, proposed by Congress, and ratified by the Legislatures of the several States, pursuant to the fifth Article of the original Constitution.

Note: The following text is a transcription of the first ten amendments to the Constitution in their original form. These amendments were ratified December 15, 1791, and form what is known as the "Bill of Rights."

Amendment I

---

[183] U.S. National Archives and Records Administration, "The Charters of Freedom: The Bill of Rights,"
http://www.archives.gov/exhibits/charters.

Congress shall make no law respecting an establishment of religion, or prohibiting the free exercise thereof; or abridging the freedom of speech, or of the press; or the right of the people peaceably to assemble, and to petition the Government for a redress of grievances.

Amendment II
A well regulated Militia, being necessary to the security of a free State, the right of the people to keep and bear Arms, shall not be infringed.

Amendment III
No Soldier shall, in time of peace be quartered in any house, without the consent of the Owner, nor in time of war, but in a manner to be prescribed by law.

Amendment IV
The right of the people to be secure in their persons, houses, papers, and effects, against unreasonable searches and seizures, shall not be violated, and no Warrants shall issue, but upon probable cause, supported by Oath or affirmation, and particularly describing the place to be searched, and the persons or things to be seized.

Amendment V
No person shall be held to answer for a capital, or otherwise infamous crime, unless on a presentment or indictment of a Grand Jury, except in cases arising in the land or naval forces, or in the Militia, when in actual service in time of War or public danger; nor shall any person be subject for the same offence to be twice put in jeopardy of life or limb; nor shall be compelled in any criminal case to be a witness against himself, nor be deprived of life, liberty, or property, without due process of law; nor shall private property be taken for public use, without just compensation.

Amendment VI
In all criminal prosecutions, the accused shall enjoy the right to a speedy and public trial, by an impartial jury of the State and district wherein the crime shall have been committed, which district shall have been previously ascertained by law, and to be informed of the nature and cause of the accusation; to be confronted with the witnesses against him; to have compulsory process for obtaining witnesses in his favor, and to have the Assistance of Counsel for his defence.

Amendment VII

In Suits at common law, where the value in controversy shall exceed twenty dollars, the right of trial by jury shall be preserved, and no fact tried by a jury, shall be otherwise re-examined in any Court of the United States, than according to the rules of the common law.

Amendment VIII
Excessive bail shall not be required, nor excessive fines imposed, nor cruel and unusual punishments inflicted.

Amendment IX
The enumeration in the Constitution, of certain rights, shall not be construed to deny or disparage others retained by the people.

Amendment X
The powers not delegated to the United States by the Constitution, nor prohibited by it to the States, are reserved to the States respectively, or to the people.

Note: The capitalization and punctuation in this version is from the enrolled original of the Joint Resolution of Congress proposing the Bill of Rights, which is on permanent display in the Rotunda of the National Archives Building, Washington, D.C.